MTG

MTG

Marjorie Taylor Greene

This book is dedicated to my father, Robert David Taylor. A forgotten American who never finished college, he served in the Vietnam War and became a millionaire through hard work because he lived the American dream.

"Marjorie Taylor Greene has been one of the most fierce warriors in Congress for America First and all it stands for. Despite the onslaught of attacks from the Marxist Democrats and Fascists in the Media, Marjorie refuses to back down and never stops fighting. She stands with the PEOPLE, NOT THE POLITICIANS. Her America First credentials are forged in steel, and with fighters like her, we will Make America Great Again."

—President Donald J. Trump

CONTENTS

FOREWORD

Since elected, Marjorie's home has been swatted, and her family—my grandchildren—have been attacked and harassed in public and online. Marjorie's own life has been threatened. I always knew it would be hard for my daughter when she was elected to Congress. But I didn't realize just how tough these past few years would be.

I will tell you firsthand, it's always those closest to the ones being attacked who take it the worst. That pain and worry is multiplied when the person on the receiving end is your child. Despite it all, Marjorie has always kept fighting, refusing to back down.

You probably know Marjorie as the outspoken firebrand who speaks her mind and isn't afraid to speak the truth. I know her as the little girl who changed my life on May 27, 1974.

When Marjorie was born, her father Bob and I had $500 to our name, tucked under the bedroom rug. During the Jimmy Carter years, we lived in rental houses and apartments, trying to save and keep up with inflation (sound familiar?). Twice, we had just enough gas money to get to Bob's parents' house in Michigan, where we slept on the sofa bed until we could figure out our next move (sleeping on a sofa bed can be really motivating!). It was tough for us, like so many other families. We didn't have much, but we had each other. We had our family.

Bob worked hard; I mean really hard to provide for our family. After years of trying to find steady work in construction, he decided to go out and start his own business. Over the years, through hard work, grit, and determination, Bob built a thriving business in the state of Georgia and eventually built the house on the lake we called home for years to come. And with Marjorie's little brother joining us two years after she was born, we were truly living the American Dream.

Marjorie was always a "daddy's girl." She had Bob wrapped around her finger. I wasn't close to my own father, but watching Bob and Marjorie's relationship was everything I dreamt of with my own dad . . . I look back and am so thankful for those memories. He was the most precious father. And he always pushed Marjorie one step further in whatever she did. Sometimes, I thought his pushing went a little too far. But now I know Bob's insistence is exactly what helped prepare her for the battles to come.

Shortly after Marjorie was elected, Bob passed away from cancer. You can imagine, on top of the relentless attacks, smears, and falsehoods by the Democrats, media, and people online, this was a very difficult time for our family. The man who led our family, the man who poured blood, sweat, and tears to put a roof over our heads and food on our table, had gone to be with his Creator.

Throughout the treatments, hospital visits, and in-home hospice care, Marjorie was right there with us, clenching her father's hand as he neared the end of his life, just as he had clenched hers in the hospital 47 years before.

To the public eye, she remained the strong, fierce woman that you have come to know. She had to—for her kids and for me. But I knew the loss of her dad pained her deeply. During that difficult time, I knew the Lord was arming her for the battles you and I see her face every single day in the Halls of Congress.

Since the day my husband died, life has been difficult. With inflation and rising costs, I decided to downsize and sell our family home of 35 years, which my love Bob built for us. Not only that, the price of utilities and gas has gone through the roof, and we all know it is scary to even plan on your next trip to the grocery store.

I have many senior friends who are on a fixed income that barely covers the cost of what they need, much less want. It is heartbreaking to know a holiday is coming up and you know people who can't afford to buy presents for their grandchildren. Even milk, butter, and meat have become expensive luxuries.

On top of the financial struggles those of us on fixed incomes face, I see the very fabric of American values threatened: Our culture is threatened by wokeness, where boys are told they are girls, where young children are being taught sick graphic sex lessons in schools by groomers, and where people are told they are bad just because they happen to be white.

Every day, it is harder to recognize the America in which we raised our children. But Marjorie is on the frontlines, refusing to stay silent, always speaking the truth, and fighting back—the way only a mother knows how.

Bob and I raised Marjorie to speak her mind and speak the truth. That's too much for some people, and that's okay. There are too many politicians out there who just say what they think people want to hear. I'm proud of my daughter, Marjorie Taylor Greene, a woman in politics who breaks the mold, moves public opinion, and has been one of the most effective members of Congress in anyone's memory.

The fight for the heart and soul of our country and a return to God is too important. And I'm so thankful I live in a country with a fighter in Congress like my daughter, Marjorie Taylor Greene.

—Delle Taylor

1

Blue Jeans and Big Dreams

EVERYONE HAS THEIR FAVORITE PAIR of blue jeans.

We have our preferred brands and go-to styles. You can wear them to school, a date night, a game, a party, a dance, or to work, whether you're changing the oil under a lifted truck on the job site or going into the office. You can even wear them to church. Some of us slide them on while standing up, balancing from one foot to the other; others wiggle into them while lying on the bed, sucking in to zip up the zipper and button the waist.

Blue jeans are a staple for all Americans at all times.

And no matter who you are, that favorite pair fits just right and feels so good. Once you have them on, you are unstoppable. That's what it feels like to be an American. Unstoppable. Or at least that's what it *used* to feel like to be American.

I'm telling you about blue jeans because decades ago, when big corporations took their manufacturing overseas, those iconic blue jeans we wear began arriving from nearly every country *but* America. With their cheaper labor costs, India, Mexico, China, and others could make them for so much less. This meant corporations selling American labels discovered they could make more money buying denim manufactured overseas. Like with so many other industries, globalist, America-last policies have decimated the textile industry, and American manufacturers, one by one, have died out.

At the time of this writing, the district I represent in Georgia is home to one of only two remaining factories in the United States making classic denim jeans with actual blue indigo dye. The factory in Trion, Georgia, like the entire manufacturing industry in our country, is hanging by a thread.

This factory is a perfect example of an American manufacturer hanging on and finding ways to compete with the global economy. As the primary employer in their area, the taxes this company pays, which are based on their revenue from denim and other fabrics, supply roughly *80%* of the tax base in the county. In other words, this factory pays for 80% of the area's public schools, water treatment, fire department, law enforcement, and other important services the entire county depends on. It's easy to imagine what would happen if this factory closed down and joined the graveyard of factories littered across America.

A Portrait of America

Most of rural America once looked like Trion, Georgia, with a factory providing jobs and supporting much of the infrastructure through taxes on their revenue and supplying quality, American-made goods. Workers then bought goods and services and, in turn, paid taxes. In short, factories like these made America's economy number one in the world and were the strength and security for small-town America.

Gradually, over the past fifty years, Washington, DC, has partnered with big corporations, and together, they've created trade policies that sold Americans out. America's manufacturing steadily went overseas, and as the factories began to shutter, so did our jobs, resulting in pure devastation for American families.

Let me paint a picture of what this devastation looked like for many Americans as the factories closed. Dad worked at the factory, and even though he did not hold a college degree, he earned a living wage and, as the traditional breadwinner, supported the entire family. Feeling defeated and discouraged, Dad was forced to look for a new job—and in hard economic times, we all know that's a challenge. He often couldn't find one, but when he did, it usually didn't pay enough, which meant Mom had to go to work, too, or they just had to do without. They lost their security, spending power, cars, and maybe even their house. Then Mom and Dad fought about money all the time, and perhaps in despair, Dad started drinking. Marriage, money, and alcohol problems erupted into desperate families that had to relocate to search for hope.

Their son or daughter enlists in the military, seeking opportunity, and is sent to fight in a foreign war on the other side of the world, where they get injured. Whether in their body, mind, or both, they sustain injuries and are never the same. They return home with PTSD, addictions to painkillers, or suicidal thoughts only to find that veteran's benefits leave them under-resourced and without prospects.

Multiply this across hundreds, if not thousands, of other families, and suddenly, the entire tax base of the town or county collapses.

When a factory, like our real denim manufacturer in Trion, Georgia, disappears from a community, it creates a domino effect. Without their contributing tax dollars, essential public services are discontinued or underfunded. Next, new industries don't move in because of the lack of infrastructure and increased poverty, which means no new jobs are created. If new businesses do open, they often don't last long as the people in the community can't afford to spend money there. Aside from a few essentials, like a gas station, that can hang on, the once-vibrant town is now a shell of its former self. Broken and poverty-stricken, the entire community and many individual families are decimated by the loss of a factory.

Why does this happen? Politicians and bureaucrats in DC enacted policies that promoted a big, global economy and served corporate greed, empowering them to make the cheapest possible goods at the lowest labor costs to maximize shareholder profits. As a result, these policies have gutted rural America. The men and women in Washington have absolutely *no* idea what it's like in these towns or how to manage the American people's tax money. They've never had to make the smart decisions or hard calls necessary to survive in business, resulting in them racking up over $32 *trillion* of debt. Their America-last policies have destroyed small-town USA by eliminating our manufacturing base and taking American families with it.

Once we lose those factories and jobs, they never really come back. Nowadays, you can drive all over the country and see gutted towns with closed factories. They're like skeletons, reminiscent of an America that was booming, strong, and growing, paying our people to *work* and promoting traditional values.

That America, the one I love, is all but gone. It's hanging by a thread . . .

Or is it?

The factory in Trion has survived on hard work, grit, and tenacity. For example, they've expanded what they produce; instead of just blue jeans, they now make fire-resistant work clothes for the oil industry (which liberals have also targeted for extinction because of their climate-change insanity). But the folks in Trion honestly don't like me talking about them. They're proud people and want to make it on their own, just like the other hardworking Americans I represent in Georgia and around the country. Many are uncomplicated, down-to-earth people with good common sense. They don't give up, don't want a handout, and will keep trying, innovating, and fighting every step of the way to preserve the way of life that their parents and grandparents made possible.

America-last policies have tried time and again to strip these people of their dignity, resources, and freedoms. And, despite all the stupid things Washington DC has done, Americans continue to hang on, endure, and find ways to thrive. Call me a hopeless romantic, but I believe in these people—because I am one of them.

A Tradition of Hard Work

My family and I lived the American dream even when it seemed part of a nightmare. I certainly wasn't born with a silver spoon in my mouth, nor were my parents, but we're a success story. We made it thanks to lots of hard work and no small number of tough choices.

My dad, Bob, met my mom, Delle, in college. Dad had already served in the Vietnam War and was a combat veteran in the Navy. He was attending Northern Michigan University, paying his way by doing construction work, when he met my mom, just a young freshman attending Wesleyan College. They hit it off immediately, got married, and dropped out of school, getting an early start on a family and an abrupt introduction into the adult world.

It was the 1970s, and America was embroiled in many controversies, including a deep recession with high inflation. Dad struggled to find steady construction work, and eventually, he started his own business, Taylor Construction Company. My mom was only nineteen when I was born on May 27, 1974, just a year after *Roe v. Wade* had made abortion legal in America. While many young women her age were entrenched in the feminist movement and pursuing college and careers, my mother chose to become a mom instead, and I have always admired her more than she knows because of that.

My father jumped in wholeheartedly and was involved in every aspect of my care, whether it was cooking breakfast before school, taking me to job sites, coaching my teams, or telling the greatest bedtime stories of all time. He provided me with a resolute assurance of one of the most powerful forces in the world: a father's love. Mom and Dad also provided me with my best friend, my brother David, who was born two years after me.

When I was born, my parents didn't have much money, only $500 rolled up in aluminum foil hidden under a rug. They didn't have insurance, either, so they paid out of pocket for the whole hospital bill. In fact, growing up, we were so poor we ended up moving thirteen times, from apartments to rental houses and not one trailer but two. All the while, Dad looked for work and mastered the requirements of owning a business—bidding the jobs, sourcing the materials, and eventually hiring reliable helpers. When I turned fifteen, my father built our house.

Thanks to the failures of Jimmy Carter, I lived out my early childhood during hard economic times in America. But I'll forever be grateful for how my parents talked about everything in front of us kids as they navigated each challenge that was thrown their way. Whether around the table during a meal or riding in the car, they constantly discussed what was happening in our country and how it affected our family and our company. My parents kept an eye on politics; they understood it was a matter for a small business. As Washington's idiotic policies made it harder on small businesses, my parents would stay one step ahead of problems. They watched the news, and they knew how they needed to vote.

We discussed the family business a lot—problems on job sites, hiring and firing, managing the money, and more. I soaked it all up, and, as a result, my understanding of politics and business was founded at our dinner table. Little did we know at the time how much I'd end up needing it! Thanks, Mom and Dad!

As you can imagine, they talked about money *a lot*, mainly because, in the beginning, we had so little. If they were going to make it, they had to be incredibly strategic with what we did have. Don't get me wrong—these weren't academic conversations, and they didn't always agree. They had debates, and yes, sometimes arguments, about what to do, but they *worked it out*.

As I sat in on these conversations, I naturally became the "why" kid—you know, the one always asking one annoying question after another. I was hungry to *understand*. As my parents patiently answered my many questions, I began to understand the world around me. But, more importantly, I was learning about the family business and how it was affected by the economy, which was influenced by politics.

By far, the biggest lesson my dad taught me in business is that the customer is *king*. You served your customers when you did an excellent job, provided excellent service, and offered an excellent product.

With everything in them, Mom and Dad believed that whatever you do, do it right, and if you mess up, *make* it right. Everything was always done to the customer's satisfaction *before* asking for payment because that was how one built a good reputation and stayed in business. From school to working in the family business to running the family and eventually serving as a member of Congress, this lesson of serving with excellence was ingrained in me. I have taken it with me on every step of my journey.

Building the Future

Before I knew it, I was off to college at the University of Georgia. While there, I met Perry Greene, and—like my mom—we married young. I was just a baby of twenty-one. Perry, using his accounting degree, found a job auditing for Ernst and Young. I was the first person in my family to graduate from college (remember, my parents dropped out to become . . . well . . . parents) and earned a business degree. After graduating, I didn't go to one single interview—instead, I chose to bring what I'd learned home and went to work for Taylor Construction Company.

I dove into working in accounts payable and receivable, where I learned another valuable lesson: If you want to understand the inner workings of a business, do the books! Yet anyone who has ever been involved in a family business understands that you never do *just one job*! You do everything, from answering the phone to running supplies to a job site to even unclogging the toilet when the need arises.

After a few years, my parents were ready to retire, so Perry and I developed a proposal to buy Taylor Construction Company. That's right; they didn't give it to us, we had to *buy* it. A legal contract was prepared, signed, and we spent years paying them off. In 2002, we became the owners of Taylor Construction.

When you own a small business, you intimately understand how *everything* affects your business because your business is not just your livelihood; it's your *life*. Interest rates would affect our customers' ability to get loans, and supply issues could easily ruin a job. For example, if the price of lumber or another material skyrocketed after a bid was submitted and the contract had been signed, we were on the hook for the additional costs. The labor force, the weather, or a pandemic are all factors that can threaten your small business's existence.

During the recession of 2009, many of our construction company competitors went out of business. Some friends and subcontractors in related industries didn't make it either, and it was also brutal on Taylor Construction. We'd gone through many growth phases, and, in 2009, we found our company was too big to survive. We had to make tough decisions about who would stay and who we had to let go. There's nothing worse than laying off someone you know and value simply because you can't afford to keep them—all while not knowing if they'll be able to find more work.

We ran Taylor as we witnessed companies around us disappear due to America-last policies. Local suppliers, from whom we bought materials, went out of business because they couldn't compete in a global market. They'd sourced their materials locally to buy American, but cheaper materials from overseas meant they couldn't compete on price, and *boom*! Window manufacturers, makers of siding, and suppliers of roofing material were all gone! And with it went their jobs and the hopes of finding a new one. Taylor Construction could have been among those names, but somehow, we survived through God's grace and lots of hard work.

Forgotten Americans. That's what I call many Americans who were failed by the America-last policies passed in Washington. They're the factory workers left jobless when their work went overseas, those who lost their jobs in recessions, and those who had their lives destroyed during the pandemic because of communist-like shutdown policies and forced COVID-19 vaccine requirements.

They're regular people like you and me—you know, the ones without a golden parachute, and our government has failed them. They didn't have trust funds, they worked hard for everything they had, and they lived for their jobs or small businesses just like we did . . . only to find it still wasn't enough.

Just look at the entire American steel industry. Andrew Carnegie, one of the wealthiest and most generous men in history, made a great deal of his fortune through steel. Unfortunately, globalism all but destroyed American steel. While it revitalized a little under President Trump, America-last policies made it nearly impossible for the United States steel to compete against places like China, utterly devastating a once-vibrant industry.

I also experienced the impact of regulations firsthand. As a small business owner, I had to be good at managing people and also become a *master* at handling red tape in order to survive. Believe me when I say I am an advocate for safety and best practices, but the federal government puts so many senseless, stifling regulations on American businesses.

During the COVID shutdown, as a construction company, we were classified as essential, but the government employees who were supposed to inspect our sites weren't working. All work ground to a halt, and there was nothing we could do for our customers or our employees. We were supposed to be able to work and keep our people employed, but because the government was shut down, so were we.

The shutdown for COVID was arguably the first time we embraced communism in America—extremist policies imported along with a virus straight from China.

As I write this, I'm on the COVID Select Subcommittee investigating COVID's origins and our government's role in using tax dollars to fund gain-of-function research on this deadly virus. Once called xenophobic and dismissed by the so-called "experts," many details conclusively paint a picture of this virus's origins and mishandling. However, I'll spend more time on COVID later.

The combination of bad decisions (like the ones our government made regarding COVID), globalist policies which relegated many to Forgotten Americans, and inexperienced politicians who'd never run a successful company have all damaged this once-great land of opportunity. But a few have fought back tenaciously, survived, and found ways to thrive through each challenge—one of whom inspired me to run for Congress!

Make America Great Again

President Trump was the first politician who made sense to many Forgotten Americans because he didn't talk like a politician. Watching Donald J. Trump, then just a successful American businessman on the 2015-2016 Republican Presidential Primary stage, standing out and outshining sixteen other seasoned political candidates was thrilling to me, and I wasn't alone. For the first time in a long time, a man was running for office who stood for our beliefs, spoke like a regular person, and championed the America-first policies that so many of us believe in—despite the fact that even the Republican party had not stood for them in years.

We elected President Trump because he stood out in all the right ways. He understood us and how America-last Washington had sold us out. For the first time, we heard a man with an incredible record of real-life success explain a plan to Make America Great Again. He declared that he would drain the swamp of all the corruption and rot that engulfed Washington in every department of the federal government. President Trump stood against the never-ending foreign wars that America forced its way into, where we sent our loved ones to fight for another country's border, only to return home wounded, scarred, or in a flag-draped coffin. He spoke on debate stages, at rallies, and on his famous Twitter account about creating a better tax plan, stopping government-run healthcare, cutting the massive amount of red tape and regulations strangling businesses, bringing back American manufacturing, stopping China, rebuilding our military after Obama policies weakened it, and, most of all, building a wall to defend America's border from a daily invasion of unknown people and an unknown amount of drugs.

Then, as President, he signed into law the Tax Cuts and Jobs Act, which helped all income brackets but especially the middle-class and working-class Americans. IRS data shows the effects of tax credits and other reforms to the tax code: filers with an adjusted gross income (AGI) of $15,000 to $50,000 received the greatest benefit of a tax cut of 16-26% in 2018. Filers who earned $50,000 to $100,000 received a 15-17% tax cut, and those earning $100,000 to $500,000 saw their personal income taxes cut by approximately 11-13%. The wealthy who earned more than $1 million per year saw less than 6%. This was exactly the *opposite* of what Democrats claimed, saying that President Trump's tax plan would only help the rich, like him.

For us at Taylor Construction, the business tax cuts enabled us to reinvest in our business and provide bonuses to our employees. Many American companies benefited because we kept more of the money we worked so hard to earn. This extra money, in companies' as well as peoples' pockets, increased spending power, drove growth, and created economic stability. And most importantly, it gave us all hope for the future.

Sadly, America is in danger of losing President Trump's Tax Cuts and Jobs Act, which is set to expire in 2025 after the next presidential election. And I can tell you for a fact that if we have a Democrat-controlled White House again, we can expect Democrats to raise taxes because that is all they talk about. Democrats believe that Washington has a revenue problem, when in reality, we all know that it's not a revenue problem; Washington has a spending problem.

Real-Life Experience

I may only have a bachelor's degree in business administration, but it's fair to say I have a Ph.D. in reality! Owning and operating a business will teach you more lessons than the greatest colleges and universities in the world—there is simply no comparison. The same lessons imparted to me as a second generation entrepreneur, a committed business owner, and a servant to my community are what we need more of in Washington.

As a business owner, you must solve the problems that no one else can. You are always the last to get paid. This means you must pay the company bills and payroll before you can even think about paying yourself. You, and only you, are the one who is responsible at all times and legally liable under the weight of the law, no matter how much insurance you have.

During bad economic times, you stay up at night thinking about what you have to do to survive and ensure you can pay all of your employees. You understand you aren't just responsible for feeding your own kids—you're responsible for feeding all your employees' kids and keeping a roof over their heads, too. Our fiscally responsible decisions and dedication to excellent customer service set Taylor Construction above the rest and helped us survive tough economic downturns.

I truly believe that the same approach can be applied to government. Congress must take a fiscally conservative approach to the budget, start treating the American people like customers, and provide them with excellent customer service. Excellent customer service to the American people is exactly how we can begin saving this country. Excellent customer service builds trust, provides solutions to problems, and, most of all, makes customers—the American people—happy!

Our government has served itself, not the people, which is the opposite of what our Founding Fathers imagined for our country. We must return to a better way of running our government because our country faces many enemies, both inside and outside. The good news is that Americans are great people and understand how to work hard. It's time for all of us to fight back, just as President Trump did!

Now, I will stand with anyone who is like-minded and who will stand up against the communists in the Democrat party, the predators who want to sexualize and mutilate our children, the climate alarmists who threaten our nation's future, and the Deep State trying to forever take power out of the hands of the American people.

In the pages of this book, we're going to take a look behind the veil together, and I'm going to tell you a few things you might not know. Some of it is bleak and frightening, but I will tell you this: I have hope for America. I believe we can be great again and that our best days are ahead of us. If we come together, defy apathy, vote, and continue America's tradition of hard work and values, we can take our country back. I will not let them silence my voice or that of the American people.

2

January 6

On January 3, 2021, I was sworn into office, and the next day, on January 4, 2021, I flew on Air Force One with President Trump. I was honored to accompany President Trump to hold a rally in my district in Dalton, Georgia. The Georgia Senate seat election was the very next day, and we were giving one last push to save it. I was in awe of President Trump. Despite being under so much pressure that comes with serving as President and working to try to uncover election fraud from the November 2020 election, here he was, giving an all-out push to get out the vote for Georgia.

Before I was sworn in as a freshman in Congress, I began the effort to object to Joe Biden's nomination. Beginning in December, I was busy organizing in the lead up to January 6. I was constantly on the phone with other Republican members of Congress, planning our objection to Joe Biden's election—a grassroots response fueled by rampant irregularities and questions about the 2020 election.

Many didn't realize it, but this objection to the electoral votes was the same thing Democrats had done to the past three Republican presidents. In 2016, Representatives Sheila Jackson Lee and Barbara Lee led a failed objection to President Trump's victory. Before that, Senator Barbara Boxer objected to President George W. Bush's second electoral win in 2005, which came four years after the Congressional Black Caucus objected to President Bush's first win. The only difference between the Democrat objections and ours was that we had massive numbers and Senators involved. Many more members of Congress and Senators objected than had been seen before. I believe Democrats could see our efforts and the resulting momentum and were terrified that we could be successful. You see, if both chambers have the numbers to question the electoral votes for a state, those votes are not counted. And we thought we had enough to challenge in a few key states.

Matt Gaetz and I had been assigned to handle the debate over Michigan. The amount of work to prepare for this was unreal, and we had worked tirelessly. As the debate began, with the first state on our list, Arizona, our session was suddenly interrupted.

The sergeant at arms announced the House floor was under lockdown!

We on the House floor had no idea what was going on outside the Capitol. I was utterly shocked by the riot that spun out of the January 6 protests. I simply couldn't believe it, and while everyone else in America was watching it on TV, we had no idea what would happen that day.

In the middle of a lawful debate, we were presented with a choice: leave now and try to get back to our offices and staff on our own or stay while they locked down the chamber to defend it. As a brand-new member of Congress, I wasn't sure I could find my way back to my office on my own . . . so I decided to stay.

As we began to access news of the riot, we immediately thought that a group like Antifa was behind it, as Antifa and BLM riots were the only violent ones we had ever seen. In the years leading up to 2020, our country has heard the Democrats and the media call violent riots from groups like those "peaceful protests" as they burned, looted, and attacked law enforcement. So, our natural assumption was that more left-wing violence was happening at the Capitol.

It has since come out from videos that not only Antifa and provocateurs but many federal agents and undercover agents were in the crowd. At the time, we had no idea that Trump supporters got wrapped up in the Capitol breach, only that they were there peacefully protesting.

Many of us decided to stay in the House chamber, while the Secret Service swept away Nancy Pelosi, Mike Pence, and other top leaders. Those of us who remained were on our own with just a handful of sergeants at arms.

As we hunkered down, we heard a gunshot. I would later learn that it was Ashli Babbitt being murdered just outside the speaker's lobby. The House chamber erupted into a mass of confusion, and I witnessed first-hand the difference between how Democrats and Republicans handled the threat. From the moment we became aware of the riots, the difference between the parties became crystal clear. While the Democrats reacted in weakness and cowardice, our nation's Republican members of Congress earned my respect by responding with courage. Many of the Democrats were simply going crazy! Some were outrageous. Most of the Republicans were calmer and more level-headed. We were all assuming we were under attack from the same violent rioters that nearly burned down Washington and almost broke the security barricade in an attempt to kill President Trump at the White House.

As supporters of the Second Amendment of the Constitution, some members carried concealed weapons and were ready to be good guys with guns, defending themselves and others if need be. Some created weapons from items around them, like the stand from a hand sanitizer dispenser or broken-off pieces of furniture on the House floor. They were ready to protect us and our House.

This is where I first met Congressman Clay Higgins from Louisiana. "I don't know what's going on," I told him. I'm 5'2" and not very big, have never engaged in any physical violence, and have definitely never been involved in anything like this before. I was terrified, thinking that the same people we saw on TV night after night attacking police officers had just breached the Capitol.

Clay reassured me, "I'm going to stick right by your side. You go with me." He was one of the armed Republican members of Congress exercising his Second Amendment rights that day. I'd never thought much about it before that, but we constantly deal with death threats, and it's right and appropriate for members of Congress to be able to carry a gun, even on the House floor. Clay is a former member of law enforcement, and I trust men like him to protect themselves—and others—responsibly with a gun.

When Clay said he'd look out for me, I breathed a prayer of thanks to God that someone of integrity recognized how afraid I was and was willing to step up to protect me. Clay still knows how grateful I am for him that day because I've told him so many times!

When tear gas was deployed inside the Capitol, we were instructed to reach under our chairs where emergency kits were stored. Within each kit was a ventilator device with an electric fan that provided oxygen as soon as you pulled the hood out. The plastic was so thick that I couldn't see through it, and at that moment, I realized I couldn't smell anything. It didn't seem wise to put that thing on my head. If I had to run for safety or were attacked, I'd be in the worst position possible—unable to see or hear over the fan. Many of the Democrats obligingly put theirs on and some were lying on the floor, hysterical.

The House chamber was in complete and utter disarray.

At one point, the crowd had begun banging on the door, loudly trying to push the door open. Finally, the military and police showed up, decked out in full equipment and armed with rifles. Boy, were we glad to see them! We were very grateful to have help to get to a safe location.

One of the soldiers declared, "We're going to get y'all out of here." They had a plan, but several of the Republican Congressmen said, "We're going to stay right here and defend the House chamber." As they began barricading the door with furniture, I noticed not one Democrat was willing to stay to defend the chamber.

The sergeant at arms and Capitol Police had planned escape routes to direct members of Congress to safety through secret passageways in case of an attack on the Capitol. The soldiers ushered us out in a group, which quickly became chaos as they led us downstairs, down hallways and stairs, trying to keep us safely away from the protesters. But protesters were everywhere, and they had to change our path multiple times.

I ended up losing Clay as we ran—literally *ran*—down the halls. I saw that it was a problem that so many of our representatives were older and physically unable to run. How do you get them to safety when they cannot move quickly because of age, physical ailments, or lack of physical fitness? Oh, and many were hysterical, with the plastic bags over their heads in fear of tear gas and the little electric fans running so they couldn't hear, either. Just imagine Jerry Nadler trying to run for safety!

It was a *disaster.* I couldn't believe the absolute chaos.

The Capitol was supposedly one of the safest places in our country, but that was proven wrong when a group of people took over the Capitol and exposed just how vulnerable it was.

I later learned that the Speaker of the House at the time, Nancy Pelosi, had failed to secure the Capitol by not bringing in the National Guard in the weeks leading up to January 6, 2021. Even worse, she had her daughter, a filmmaker, there to capture the day's events. What a great coincidence they just happened to be filming a documentary.

Sure enough, only a few people breached the Capitol, while most just walked in through open doors—making one of the biggest mistakes of their lives!

Unusually Cruel

The people who just walked through open doors are now being prosecuted—often based on who they voted for, the hat they were wearing, the flag they held, and the fact that they believed in their First Amendment freedom of speech. For the first time in American history, we have seen the political persecution of American citizens. This has been a nightmare all its own.

Congress is to have full oversight over the District of Columbia; it's funded through Congress. As members of Congress, we can tour anywhere in the District and be let in. I sent letters to the mayor, Muriel Bowser, demanding access to inspect the jail, which were largely ignored. The mayor of DC refused access to me and several other members for nearly a *year.* Congressional colleagues of mine, including Louie Gohmert, Matt Gaetz, Paul Gosar, and I were denied entry multiple times—and we were called trespassers by jail employees.

Despite our persistent efforts, it wasn't until November 4, 2021, that I was able to tour the DC jail for over three hours. And, even then, they stonewalled, delayed, and played every other cheap trick in the book to keep us out. They gave us only fifteen minutes to arrive for the tour and even tried to block us from seeing the January 6 defendants. But eventually, we got access.

What we saw was nothing short of cruel and unusual punishment.

In my report of our findings from this tour, titled *Unusually Cruel*—which you can find online—I detail what we saw in the jail. We witnessed many disturbing things, but for this purpose, let's stick with the roughly forty inmates housed there for January 6-related charges and the inhumane conditions in which they're being held.

As we tried to gain access to the section where the January 6 defendants were being held, we were told no and that our tour was over. I responded, "No, the tour's *not* over. The whole point was to see the whole jail and the January 6 defendants." They tried to stonewall us again while claiming they had nothing to hide. "If there's nothing to hide," I countered, "then we should be seeing it."

It was a *fight*, a constant rolling argument with the puppets on site and the bosses pulling the strings. I stood my ground, determined to get back there, and, once I did, it became obvious why they didn't want to let us see the J6 defendants.

The J6 defendants were held in a previously closed down section of the jail. The cells were small, often with just a toilet, sink, and cot. In my report, I describe, "The walls of the rooms had residue of human feces, bodily fluids, blood, dirt, and mold. The community showers were recently scrubbed of black mold, some of which remained."[1] U.S. Marshals had recently inspected the area and written a damning report about the jail. So, the warden made the pre-trial J6 defendants scrub and clean before we visited.

As the inmates noticed our presence, about forty of them began to flood forward with hopeless eyes. Many were crying, and one even asked to hug me! Then, they formed a line to shake our hands, chants of "U-S-A" ringing out.

Defendants revealed their lack of access to their attorneys, families, or even proper nutrition while being held. Every single one of the men I saw that day were PRE-TRIAL! Not one had been convicted of any crime yet they were denied bond and held as political prisoners. In addition to the lack of access to their attorneys, they were also denied religious services, and even basic hygiene like haircuts. Instead of a prison barber trimming their hair, they were given a liquid product, Nair, which dissolves hair. They were told to rub this on their heads and faces. Many were held in solitary confinement all but a few hours a day, which was an improvement over *twenty-three* hours a day when they arrived! In the brief few hours they were let out of the cells each day, they were made to choose between going outside, calling family, calling their attorneys, or taking showers. One defendant shared that he had been in solitary confinement for two hundred days, at first twenty-three hours a day, and then reduced to *"just"* twenty-two! The air circulation was so bad that human feces polluted the air. Medical care was spotty; from a broken finger to pre-existing conditions such as celiac disease and others, no one received proper care. In the case of Leroy Coffman, who was seventy-one at the time, his forearm had turned purple and his thumb *black*. Fellow inmates feared he'd lose his arm because he had been denied medical treatment.

In the wake of their lack of access to religious and legal services, the defendants held their own religious services. Some tried to represent themselves legally, writing dozens of pages of legal motions—with no access to a law library—on notebook paper. They were treated like *prisoners of war*, one sharing that he was punched in the gut for singing the national anthem. Yet they still sang "The Star-Spangled Banner" at 9:00 p.m.

In the DC Gulag, the defendants asked us to sing with them. One man held up their flag for all of us to honor. It was a hand-drawn American flag with blue and red ink on a piece of paper, and he held it high with pride. That night, they sang our national anthem with more conviction than I've ever heard in my entire life. Their voices rang out with emotion as they pledged their allegiance to the very government that was persecuting them. They sang about the country that once was, all while being locked up and persecuted by a now tyrannical government.

I encourage you to read the report personally and hear more eyewitness accounts.

Here is an excerpt of what I shared with the defendants that day:

"I was upset about the riot on January 6. I don't call it an insurrection—it wasn't—but I was upset. But I'm here because I genuinely am worried that you all are being treated poorly, and it's a human rights abuse. It's an abuse of your civil rights, and you should be presumed innocent before proven guilty. And I believe in a good justice system and that you should be treated fairly, just like the rest of the people here that I saw tonight who are being treated very well.

I think that should be extended to every single person regardless of politics or skin color or what you're being charged with. We've heard terrible things, and I want you to know that Congressman Gohmert and I have refused to back down on this issue.

The America we know is not a racist country. On the contrary, we want people to receive fairness in the justice system."

Please let me remind you that these weren't people convicted of violent crimes; they were pre-trial, convicted of nothing! In America, we are innocent until proven guilty, but these people were being held as though they'd already been convicted of violent crimes in a trial.

I thought this kind of politicization and unusual cruelty only happened in places like Russia or China or some totalitarian regime. The January 6 defendants' treatment was absolutely sickening! This should not happen in our country!

But it did.

Since I learned of the injustice at the DC jail, I have been the leading voice against the political persecution of the January 6 defendants. In the context of the riots of the years before, I believe that what is happening to American citizens, who were upset over injustice, is beyond wrong. While I do believe that each person charged deserves justice under our law, what we are seeing with J6'ers is nothing even close to fair; it's not even humane.

I have worked as hard as I can to defend these Americans' constitutional rights. But, unfortunately, the more I have learned about their treatment, the only words that came to mind were *cruel* and *inhumane*. It's revolting and un-American.

The charges leveled against them are over the top and ridiculous. Their human rights are being abused just *miles* from a Capitol that's supposed to stand for the rule of law and equal justice. Yet it has been perverted for a political agenda.

I am not involved directly in the cases of the January 6 defendants; I'm not a lawyer, and I don't think that's the right place for me. However, I can and will continue defending their rights and working against corruption and abuse within the federal government targeting them for political reasons.

One of the most atrocious aspects is they have been held in a pretrial state. As I'm writing this, many still haven't been to court. They are being held without bail—some on nonviolent charges. These are not people who fought a police officer, resisted arrest, or killed someone. They walked up the Capitol steps, entered through an open door, walked around inside while sometimes videoing themselves, and as a result, they've been charged with crimes such as trespassing and disrupting Congress. While they await trial, many are unable to see their spouses and children as they are no longer held in the DC jail but have been transferred to jails and prisons all over the United States. After my tour, the mayor of DC refused to let any more members of Congress tour the jail until Republicans took over the majority, at which point I led members of Congress from the Oversight Committee to the DC jail. Unfortunately, we don't have enough members of Congress willing to take a hard stand required to end the political persecution of J6 defendants. And while I still hear horrible stories, I am determined to exercise our rights within DC to ensure the humane treatment of these political prisoners.

Don't Lose Hope

I want to leave you with some more of the words I shared with these mistreated January 6 defendants:

"It's wrong to abuse people. We all have our civil rights, and they need to be protected. And here's something else you need to know: It's a hard time for all of you, and it's a hard time for most people, especially being incarcerated, but don't lose hope. Don't lose hope!

You know who you are, a child of God, and He loves every single one of you. He made you, formed you, and knew you before you were born, and that's the greatest gift. He's got a plan for every single one of us. You know you're not forgotten; you're appreciated. And you're loved, and your families love you. They miss you, and your friends love you. And many people talk about you and pray for you. . . . We can come through this time in our country, and hopefully, we can all come back together, and we're not divided by that."

I ended our time together by praying for them—and here, I pray for our country. We stand on the brink of losing one of the amazing facets that make America distinct, a shining beacon of light in the world. If we sacrifice equal justice under the law and presumption of innocence until someone is proven guilty by a jury of peers, we face a justice system turned on its head and politicized. Corrupted. *Ruined*.

The Democrats think their only way of winning is by locking up their political opponents. They want to put President Trump in jail for life, which is a virtual death sentence, but they have expanded their communist tactics to pursue anyone who supports him or stands in their way. Now it's everyday Americans who are held in horrible conditions for their political beliefs. Compared to over 95% of BLM rioters' charges being dropped, these people are being used as the public example of what happens when you stand up to tyranny.

This will not happen if I can prevent it.

The events of January 6 have been mischaracterized by the Democrats and their mouthpieces in the media, a circus made of the proceedings, and these people cruelly treated. It must stop! It *will* stop—for we won't rest until these people get equal justice under the law.

They will not be forgotten. I will never forget.

3

Kicked off Committees.

I NEVER INTENDED TO GO into politics; I just wanted to be a mother to my kids and run our company. Yet I continued to watch the breakdown of the rule of law, horrible injustices, and people pressured into calling deviant behavior good, and knew someone must do something. And, as that old saying goes, it's a dirty job, but somebody's got to do it! So, I stepped up because I wanted my children to inherit America as the great nation we all know it can be again. But we're going to have to fight for it!

Which is why, on January 21, 2021, I filed articles of impeachment against Joe Biden. It was the very day Biden was inaugurated President—and I filed them on the exact issues we are currently investigating in the Oversight Committee. I submitted that Joe Biden had been using his position of power to give numerous members of his family advantages in their business dealings. Specifically, his son Hunter, who had benefited from his father's position of power to make millions on corrupt business deals in foreign countries.

Previously, Hunter Biden's laptop had been panned as "Russian disinformation," which the legacy media had tried to cover up during the election. Even though Hunter had been under investigation, the media had managed to largely keep this news out of the hands of the voting public. From government interference on social media platforms such as Twitter[2] to Deep State intelligence officials signing off on the laptop as fake news,[3] this material was buried repeatedly. But it should have prevented Biden from being elected, and it absolutely should've been grounds for his impeachment since he somehow managed to get elected anyway.

The coverup was extensive and revolting. As a member of the Oversight Committee, we subpoenaed Biden family bank records with more coming—so much more! Tracking the Biden family criminal enterprise and how they were influence-peddling Joe Biden, particularly when he was vice president, has been a massive undertaking. But I was also on target back then, and it spooked the Democrats.

It was a huge deal when I filed the articles of impeachment on Biden's first day in office on January 21, 2021. And it was no coincidence that Nancy Pelosi kicked me off *all* my committees two weeks later. While she claimed it was for content posted on Facebook or other social platforms I'd made in the past, the real reason was punishment. I had the nerve to file the articles of impeachment against our corrupt president, and I was too close to the truth. So, they would do anything they could to silence me, destroy my political career before it had hardly even started, and prevent me from opposing their crooked narrative.

After being removed from my committees, I shared in a press conference, "I'm fine with being kicked off of my committees because it'd be a waste of my time." I went on to share that I didn't respect what our government had become, a case in point being the retribution I experienced for filing articles of impeachment. I couldn't respect our rampant spending, the incredible burden of debt we're putting on our children and grandchildren, and America-last policies that have outsourced our manufacturing and jobs overseas. I went on to apologize for anything I felt I may have done wrong, and I also said CNN spreads more conspiracy theories than QAnon.

I've always been a hard worker, and I wouldn't stop because Pelosi and her cronies in the media tried to annihilate my career. I declared that it was okay because now I could talk to a *whole lot* more people, and I'd put that time to good use.

Personally, I think the plan backfired on them!

On the Record

When I was kicked off my committees, the Democrat-controlled House was busy passing all of Joe Biden's ruinous agenda without a hint of resistance. Republicans weren't getting anything done on committees anyway, and they didn't care what we had to say. So, even though I was new to politics, I knew that being on a committee as a Republican didn't matter. I viewed being kicked off my committees as a strange kind of gift—the gift of time.

It was like my chains had been broken, setting me free. I could now travel the country, fighting for America-first policies and spreading the message about what Republicans *should* be doing. I traveled everywhere, gave speeches, and raised money for other candidates who would champion conservative, America-first values.

I also spent a great deal of time on the House floor simply *learning*. I learned parliamentary procedure, how bills were debated, and I attended hearings. I would often sit in on the Rules Committee as

I wanted to understand how bills made it to the House floor. I even was able to introduce amendments to bills at the Rules Committee.

Finally, the day came when I had the opportunity to put one of the most impactful lessons I had learned into action. I was sitting on the House floor watching the Republicans and Democrats debate a bill. The person sitting in the Speaker's chair—I had no idea who because they were wearing a mask—called for a voice vote on the bill. Republicans said nay, and Democrats said yea, and since Democrats were winning everything, the speaker with the mask announced that the bill had passed.

I was shocked. I had my voting card in hand, apparently unneeded. The voting card is like a driver's license with your picture, name, and other information on it, and we're supposed to use it in a little machine to record the vote, but this vote didn't need that card. I was also surprised because there were about five Republicans on one side of the room and five Democrats on the other—out of the 435 members of Congress.

I hadn't voted. How had the bill passed? I was confused, thinking I'd missed something, and I called the Republican floor staffer over and asked about it. "What just happened?"

He told me they'd just passed a bill.

"But I didn't vote . . ." I replied.

"Oh, yes, ma'am, but most of the bills here in Congress pass by voice," he explained.

What I didn't know, until that moment, was that passing a bill by voice didn't record the individual votes, which means that there's no record of whether you voted yes or no or present—or just didn't vote. I couldn't believe it! Done this way, the American people have no record of our job performance because they can't know our voting history—which is precisely why they do it that way.

I began to ask questions, and I learned there's a parliamentary procedure that any member of Congress can use to ask for a recorded vote or roll-call vote during the debate of any bill.

And, just like that, I had a new purpose in Congress.

Since the Democrats were the ruling party, they got everything they wanted because they were all voice votes. Biden's extremist agenda was flying through the House uncontested. Nobody was doing anything to stop it or even slow it down—yet. I dedicated much of my time to sitting on the floor of the House of Representatives, watching as bills were debated, and when it came time to vote, I would call for a recorded vote.

With all my free time, I stayed on the floor for every bill I could and asked for recorded votes. It kind of became my thing, shocking representatives on both sides! The Democrats, like Nancy Pelosi and Steny Hoyer, were upset because it started messing with their schedule. They had been passing bills in record time. One after another, the bills came up and were passed by voice so they could move on to the next one. But every time I called for a recorded vote, it brought everything to a halt.

The House of Representatives had to stop while the Speaker's office sent out a call to all members of Congress to report to the House floor for the vote. Every single member of Congress was notified that we had been called on to vote. That meant everybody had to stop what they were doing; committee hearings, fundraising, lunches, and more would all cease as members of Congress made their way to vote. Jerry Nadler had to wake up from his nap and walk down to the House floor!

Nancy Pelosi had passed House rules for COVID, which resulted in each vote taking at least forty-five minutes or longer.

In comparison, as I write this, with Republicans in charge of the House, we have five-minute and sometimes even two-minute votes!

After the vote, everyone would return to what they were doing, and the House would begin debating another bill. Since I did not have to run off to a committee meeting, I would sit there, and as soon as they passed the bill by voice, I would call for a roll call vote . . . and the same process repeated all over! I was seriously throwing sand in their gears, and it made the Democrats mad!

Steny Hoyer was so upset he marched down to Kevin McCarthy's office and demanded that he make me stop. Kevin just laughed about it and said, "Well, I'm not the one who kicked her off her committees! She's got nothing to do." They, in essence, had created this situation.

For a long time, I kept this up almost by myself. But something odd began to happen; the Republicans also started getting upset, which was very interesting to me. Sure, they didn't like their schedule being interrupted, but I uncovered that many did not want their votes to be on record! With every recorded vote, everyone knows if their Representative voted yes or no on a particular bill. I learned a lot of the Republicans in Congress are actually *horrible* moderates who did not want to have their voting record on Joe Biden's agenda exposed to their constituents!

Chairwoman of the Committee of the Whole

On one side, Democrats were mad at me for slowing down Joe Biden's extremist liberal agenda, and on the other side, Republicans were chewing me out for putting them on record. In fact, one senior Republican spent nearly an hour trying to talk me out of calling for recorded votes. She flat-out explained that people did not want to be put on record and that I was making it very difficult for some of them. What she didn't know, however, is that all this opposition made me want to do it even *more!*

You see, I have this weird idea that representatives in Congress are to *serve the American people,* and they owe them a record of their job performance. So, no, of course I don't think they should be allowed to hide behind a voice vote. They owed it to their district and the entire country to have their votes recorded.

While it made many people mad, I doubled down! I decided that I was going to call for as many recorded votes as I could. Republicans shouldn't be afraid to show people their voting records, and it turns out that members of the Freedom Caucus aligned with my beliefs. They came to understand what a powerful tool it was when, at one point, I was the only person in Congress slowing down Joe Biden's agenda simply by asking for recorded votes. Together, members of the Freedom Caucus and I created a floor schedule and took turns during the entire 117th Congress, demanding recorded votes on as many bills as possible. I started an effort to make every bill as difficult on the Democrats as possible while calling my fellow Republicans to be accountable for their votes. As a result, we had over 550 bills on record.

Not only did calling for recorded votes slow down the Democrat's agenda, it also caused a few of their really bad bills to fail, such as Cori Bush's bill to allow felons to vote in our elections, including while they are in jail. Her bill had passed by voice, but luckily, I was there to call for recorded votes and forced Congress to vote for her bill. It turns out that even Democrats didn't want to vote with her for her absurd bill to allow felons to vote! The bill went down with 119 Democrats voting alongside 209 Republicans—all voting *no* against her bill. Had I not been there to force a recorded vote,

BLM Congresswoman Cori Bush's bill would have passed by voice and likely made it to Joe Biden's desk.[4]

The whole process revealed to me why Congress is so broken. I remember watching a vote pass by voice that was for over seven million dollars in spending. It passed with maybe fewer than ten members of Congress saying yes or no on the floor. I couldn't believe how irresponsibly the House was using the American people's dollars! It shocked me that so many representatives could spend Americans' hard-earned money so frivolously by simply saying yes or no without all of Congress being involved or being held accountable on the record.

I know many people who work incredibly hard, sometimes even two or three jobs. They pay their taxes and struggle to get by, and here is Congress, throwing their money around without any regard. Broken practices, such as the voice vote, have crippled us with so much debt that I'm not sure we can ever dig out from under it. And it wasn't just the other party; Republicans were also playing their role.

Since I had been kicked off all my committees, I declared myself the unofficial chairwoman of the group calling for recorded votes, which we called the Committee of the Whole. If they were going to take me off my committees, I'd make one for myself—and I don't think they liked it very much!

Consequences for Standing Up

My solo efforts in the Committee of the Whole lasted about six weeks before, thank God, the Freedom Caucus members joined me because I was spending eight to ten hours a day sitting there on the House floor by myself. The Democrats hated me, but so did half the Republicans, and I became a pariah for that session of Congress. They tried to shame me and destroy me in the media.

I felt like I had to be there when we were in session, fighting my own private war for the American people and trying to expose the corruption around me.

Everywhere I went, I was hated and scorned in Washington, DC. People yelled at me as I walked and cornered me in airports. I received regular hate mail (which has never stopped) and was attacked on social media daily, with people saying horrible things about me and what they wanted to do to me. I would trend nearly every day on Twitter because of the attacks. Meanwhile, one of the worst things imaginable was happening in my personal life—my father was dying of stage four brain cancer, which had metastasized from his untreated melanoma.

But I was doing what I thought was right. I had been elected by the people of my district, I had a job to do, and I owed them my very best. Since I wasn't serving on committees, I would do anything I could to stop Joe Biden's agenda. He and his radical Left cronies were destroying our country, and I did anything possible to slow it down. When terrible bills like the Equality Act came, I would motion to adjourn and literally stop Congress. Motioning to adjourn is rare, and many representatives will never do it. I think I motioned to adjourn around six times, just trying to slow the destruction.

Most of the people around me were career politicians, whereas I didn't look at it as a career; I already had a job. This is not how I earned my paycheck, and it wasn't something owed to me by the system. I never wanted to be in politics, but I ran for Congress because I was angry and disgusted about what was happening in our country. If I could do something to stop it, I would.

If Congress were a business, it should have filed for bankruptcy long ago because no company I have ever seen could exist the way our federal government is run. If someone were to run a business like

we run our government, they would fail, undeniably. The only reason the federal government has not collapsed is because it has control
of the Federal Reserve, can print as much money as they want, and
change the debt ceiling whenever they need more money to blow.

Career politicians don't understand how their idiotic policies
ruin the lives of Americans. Their irresponsible spending has created
insurmountable debt, and they do it all at the expense of forgotten
Americans left behind by globalist policies and America-last agendas. It must stop!

As a result of the stand I have taken, I am attacked everywhere
I go with the exception of my home district or the red states of the
country. Everywhere else, there's always some random middle-aged,
nasty, white woman who is brainwashed by the View and has nothing better to do than say horrible things to me from beneath the
mask on her face. And then there are the miserable middle-aged
white men, who must hate themselves because they've been trained
to believe their white skin and male gender is ruining everything,
who will walk by me calling me a "cunt" or "bitch." Additionally, I
don't make as much money as a member of Congress as I did when
working for my construction company. In fact, it's the biggest incon-
venience of my life.

Yet, my purpose is to do the job that needs to be done, which is
to force Congress to serve the American people with excellent customer service and run the federal government like a successful business. In spite of the attacks by miserable people, most Americans
actually agree with me about Congress. The way Congress works
is broken, and it's time for a change. I am honored to be the voice
calling for it. I have found that if we want the truth to come out, we
must step up and set the record straight.

4

Setting the Record Straight

BETWEEN JANUARY 6, CALLING FOR recorded votes, and overall being too close to the mark, I quickly angered people. As a result, I came under fire like never before. The Democrats and their allies in the legacy media embarked on a campaign to ruin my reputation and assassinate my political career. I can't count the number of lies told about me in the press. I was tried and convicted in the skewed court of public opinion, often without the opportunity to defend myself. Nancy Pelosi soon kicked me off my committees.

Some lies and misrepresentations they told were so outright insane and opposite to the truth—it simply astounded me! But one of the first and most obnoxious was about Jewish space lasers. Yes, you read that right!

Around the time I was kicked off my committees, an article came out declaring I had blamed the wildfires in California on these lasers.[5] This was something I'd once said in a sarcastic social media post years before I was elected, and it was completely misrepresented in the article. Before I knew it, "Jewish space laser" and my name began trending on Twitter. I couldn't believe it—I thought there was no way everyone would treat it as anything but the joke it was. But they didn't.

On November 17, 2018, I created a post announcing that there were seventy dead and over a thousand were missing from the horrific wildfires in California. I went on to share that I was praying for everyone involved but also wanted to focus on the "coincidences."

California had just announced that they wouldn't let PG&E, the big energy company whose ill-maintained power lines were believed to be the cause of the wildfires, fail. A perfect example of the government bailing out a big, failing company, just as we've recently seen with the bailout of some big banks. I had been researching PG&E stocks, which had tanked all week, and watched as they rallied right after California made the announcement.

During my research, I found it interesting that Roger Kimmel, who was on the board of directors for PG&E, was also vice chairman of Rothschild, Inc. I was so politically naïve I knew *nothing*—nothing more than someone who listened to talk radio. I didn't know a thing about the Rothschilds other than they were a big, wealthy family. I certainly didn't think a thing about their ethnicity or religion.

I put the Kimmel connection together with the fact that PG&E had a long history of financial contributions to Jerry Brown, the former governor of California. It was easy for me to draw a connection between the Democrat governor of California and his decision to bail out this utility provider from whom he had received tons of donations. What a coincidence, I mentioned sarcastically, that Jerry Brown had just a few months earlier signed a bill protecting PG&E,

allowing them to pass off the cost of wildfire responsibility to its customers through rate hikes and bonds![6] PG&E routinely was sued over the wildfires, but now they could pass those costs on to their customer.[7]

I wasn't done. I also mentioned the "coincidence" that the fires were burning in the same areas as the projected $77 *billion*-dollar high-speed rail project being built, clearing land for Brown's pet project, for which Dianne Feinstein's late husband, Richard Blum, was the contractor. With that much money, I quipped, we could build three southern US border walls!

I was shining a spotlight on the unholy union between the government, politicians, and big companies. Americans needed to see that these people were all in bed together, with good old boy politics making people billions on a deal where they scratched each other's backs.

Around this same time, people posted on social media that they had seen lights, like blue beams, actually starting fires, and they even had videos. When I mentioned this in my post, I was simply calling attention to these posts, even clarifying that I did not know anything about its validity. However, I did go on to draw attention to the fact that PG&E partnered with a company called Solaren on space solar generators starting in 2009, which I found fascinating. Solaren harnesses the sun's energy and then, using satellites, beams it to receivers on Earth. Cool technology, right?

But I wondered what it would look like if they *missed* the receiver. Mistakes happen, especially with new inventions. How many times did the Wright brothers crash airplanes before eventually flying? Mistakes and failures are part of new inventions and technology. So, what would it look like if they missed the receiver when they were sending the sun's energy to Earth? My post was speculation, simply asking rhetorical questions. I wondered, could it cause a fire? If it did, it wouldn't look good for Solaren, but it also wouldn't look good for their partner, PG&E.

To top it off, whoever bought PG&E stock when it was low, right before the state bailed them out, would do *incredibly* well on their investments. Of course, to get that info ahead of time, you'd need to know someone, and we've already seen there were a lot of powerful, wealthy people interconnected here.

I ended my post by saying I hoped the Solaren people had good aim!

From that post where I showed people this unholy union and sarcastically posed some uncomfortable questions, they created a political hit piece saying that I'd claimed *Jewish space lasers* had caused the fires!

Rothschild is a Jewish family, which I didn't know at the time of the post. So, they used the tired old liberal line of "racism" here to add to the misrepresentation of what I was saying. Never mind that I am the very opposite of an anti-Semite, having donated to the Temple Institute in Israel, a fund that helps rebuild the Jewish temple on the Temple Mount in Israel. There is not an antisemitic bone in my body, but they played that card in addition to the laser angle just to make sure I sounded not only like a complete idiot but also a bigot.

Although the lie-filled article came out years after my original social media post, the Left lost their minds over it. Kevin McCarthy even condemned me, along with many other Republicans. They asked me to visit the Holocaust Museum in DC so I could be "educated" about the horrors of the Holocaust—never mind that I'd actually been to Germany and seen the camps when I was a young woman! We had toured the museums, and I personally saw the disgusting gas ovens.

My Savior is a Jewish carpenter who died on the cross for my sins, and I have no antisemitic sentiments whatsoever. Yet, this article robbed me of my dignity, credibility, and chance to go to the Holy Land as a freshman in Congress. You see, the American Israel Public Affairs Committee (AIPAC) invited every freshman member of Congress to go to Israel . . . except me. I didn't get to go because of this slanderous article.

My actual social media post, which no one apparently bothered to read, said nothing antisemitic whatsoever. It was insulting that they believed this ridiculous article instead of what I'd actually written.

The article was a hit piece, pure and simple.

When you hit close to the mark, it stirs up the hornet's nest. They get scared and strike—they try to assassinate your character, ruin your career, and outright cancel you. This all happened around the same time I was removed from my committees. They needed a hit piece to try to destroy my political career, and discovered they could use a years-old post, twist my words, and make me appear like an antisemitic fool. So, instead of arguing with me about the corruption within the California government, they made up a lie about Jewish space lasers.

And people believed it. They believed it because they didn't know me. They believed it because they were part of the establishment in Washington who didn't like me making waves. I was calling attention to corruption in California, bringing the Biden family to the forefront, and, remember, I was the one who filed the impeachment documents against Joe Biden on his first day in office.

Each inflammatory article against me has been a constant attack on my character and career to get me to shut up and stop pointing out the rampant corruption in government. But I will *not* be silenced, and I refuse to let them duct tape my mouth shut. This country is too great to let the crooked bureaucrats who infest the swamp destroy it and the American people they are supposed to represent.

I've been called an antisemite more than once for attacking George Soros, who spends billions of dollars buying politicians to keep our borders open and forward his globalist Marxist insanity. Soros has his hands in so many pockets he probably can't even keep track of them all, but they have the gall to attack Clarence Thomas for not disclosing gifts.

Being called antisemitic is usually a death blow in politics. You can't survive, which is why they launched that nuclear weapon right before I was kicked off my committees and started attacking me and leveling baseless accusations. But it didn't work! Despite how freely the Left tosses around the "racist" card, thankfully, not everyone took them at their word. Orthodox Jews reached out to me, befriended me, and some even donated to my campaigns. Since then, I've spent years trying to repair the damage this defaming article and similar ones did to me.

Despite the mocking t-shirts, buttons, stickers, and other items referencing Jewish space lasers that have been sent to me , the Left's political assassins couldn't take me out. Their lies have no basis, and I don't play the usual Washington political game with special interests and lobbyists.

I simply won't let them win.

The truth of who I really am, and my voting record, proves that I am no anti-Semite. I have one of the most pro-Israel voting records in the House and, when it came time to vote for Israel's real space lasers, I voted to fund them. So, it turns out I actually support Jewish space lasers.

Dark Money

The ridiculous attacks I experienced regarding the California corruption social media post certainly aren't the only times the Left has tried to take me out. Free Speech for the People, a Democrat dark money group, wanted to get me off the ballot, so they filed a lawsuit against me. Funded through various 501(c)(3)s and outside organizations, they filed a lawsuit for my primary election in 2022, claiming I violated the insurrection clause of the Fourteenth Amendment. They needed five voters from my district, so they approached the Democrat Chair for the district, who then joined the lawsuit alongside four other Democrats.

I spent nearly a *million dollars* in legal fees to fight them, and I made history once again. As I write this, I am the only member of Congress who has sat on the witness stand under oath, accused of insurrection, and questioned about January 6. They grilled me for hours! The questioning happened just one month before my primary election in May 2022.

It was a show trial, and they looked like clowns as they spun their twisted narrative. A few things they said stood out as being dumber than the rest. First, they said I got my inspiration from *Independence Day*, a 1996 action movie featuring Will Smith. The stupid lawyer even played a clip from the movie, which he wanted to use as evidence against me!

After he played the clip, he asked me if I knew the movie. I thought maybe I'd seen it years ago with my kids, but then, with no evidence whatsoever, he started claiming that it was my favorite movie, and it's where I got my inspiration. The judge shook his head and put his face in his hands.

The lawyer made himself look like a complete idiot! The second truly absurd thing that happened during this clown show was when I was questioned about 1776. The lawyer described a social media post I published about when America issued the Declaration of Independence. The lawyer was trying to accuse me of inciting insurrection at the capitol on January 6 by using the term 1776. What he missed was that I wasn't talking about war—I was talking about our country's history of standing up to *tyrants*, men like Joe Biden. (We had objected to Joe Biden's electoral college votes, some of which I believe were fraudulent in a stolen election.)

"You mean '1776' like that?" I said, pointing to the Georgia state seal, which was mounted on the wall directly above the judge's head. I said I knew he wasn't from around here, but we have 1776 on our state seal. That arrogant New York attorney showed what an ignorant ass he really was to our Georgia courtroom.

The judge found me not guilty of inciting or planning an insurrection, and my name stayed on the ballot. Yes, it cost me nearly a million dollars in legal fees and a great deal of stress; however, it was worth it. I was not going to allow some nasty left-wing progressive group to come to Georgia and take away the rights of the people in my district to vote for me. At the end of the month, I overwhelmingly won my primary election.

Pariah No Longer

I have often been an enigma to both Democrats and Republicans, as neither seems to know what to do with me! But, during my time in office, they have learned I am sincere when I speak about corruption, the rule of law, and a genuine conservative agenda. They have called me an extreme right-wing insurrectionist, a QAnon Congresswoman—and those are the *nice* things!

But what have I said that is so extreme to them? I boldly declared that Congress failed under President Trump. We had a Republican majority, yet they didn't fund the border wall or repeal Obamacare. They didn't end abortion and instead funded Planned Parenthood for $500 million. After January 6th, I stood unapologetically supporting President Trump and would not back away from him. I would tell them to their faces that, whether they liked him or not, he was the leader of our party, and the American people supported him.

I've been labeled every hateful name in the book for wanting to secure our southern border, end the murder of innocent unborn babies, help women be mothers, protect our children from being sexualized by pedophiles, and stop life-ruining, barbaric medical procedures on minors. I've stood for America-first policies and against sending our manufacturing and jobs overseas to save a buck. I've raised the alarm over our out-of-control spending and debt, caused by both Democrats and Republicans, because no company could ever stay in business under the practices with which our country has been governed. I've argued relentlessly that America should be pushing for peace in Ukraine, not funding another foreign war defending another country's border while ours are wide open.

They've done everything they can to stop me, including "permanently" banning me from Twitter for almost the entire year of 2022 for telling the truth in a new era of censorship sponsored by big tech being in bed with a corrupt big government. I couldn't fundraise or respond to the insane attacks against me during my re-election to Congress.

The media has tried to crucify me, acting as the mouthpiece of the Democrat party, and some Republicans joined in as well. Those opposed to my down-to-earth, practical views spent the first two years of my political career trying to destroy me but failed because I had the support of the people—and because I did not back down, even when times were most challenging. No matter what, I will never stop fighting; in fact, I will fight harder than any of them can keep up with! I have traveled the country, held rallies, and made speeches everywhere possible. I have sat on the House floor, calling for recorded votes for hours on end, days at a time. I have paid outrageous legal bills and fought the lies against me that defied all truth and common sense.

Despite everything I have faced, there's one thing that tells me I'm doing the right thing: people support me. My fundraising shows it. The first quarter after they kicked me off my committees, I believe I was in the top five in the entire House of Representatives for fundraising—not because of special interests but because of ordinary Americans in my district and beyond. I've beaten them all, defeating their narrative of lies, with the help of like-minded Americans, both in politics and at home. So, you see, the voters told their representatives to support me! I stood up for them, and they told their representatives to get behind the agenda to make our country great again.

My opponents have done everything they can to eliminate me, try to kill my political career, smear me personally, and lie about my character. And it wasn't just political assassination on the agenda; I am the subject of constant death threats. A man pleaded guilty just a few months ago for planning to murder me and is awaiting his sentence as I write this. They've even tried to turn law enforcement against me! It's called "swatting." They call the police, either claiming I am suicidal or pretending it's me on the phone saying I'm suicidal and just killed someone, and the SWAT team is dispatched to my home. Seven times, once just the night before I wrote this, they called the SWAT team to my house, ready to shoot someone—*me*!

Yet, I somehow find myself one of the more politically powerful and influential members of Congress. I don't say that to brag but to show that they can't silence me. And more—they can't silence the *American people* I am sworn to represent! The people support what I'm saying because they know I am fighting for *them* and the issues they care about most!

Under a Republican Congress, I serve on three committees–Homeland Security, Oversight, and COVID Select. I'm privileged to be part of the group investigating Joe Biden for the very same issues I brought articles of impeachment against him for when he was inaugurated. I'm also part of the group shedding light on lies and misinformation spread by people like Dr. Fauci during the pandemic. We're trying to hold our government accountable for (mis) handling the whole thing and want to track down the true origins of COVID—not from a wet market, but from a Chinese lab.

Despite their attempts at political destruction, I now find myself not a pariah in the Republican party but a person who has gained the respect of many of my colleagues. I have paid my dues, literally and figuratively—one of the few to do so—to the tune of hundreds of thousands of dollars! I consider paying the NRCC dues very important; this way, I am doing my part to help other Republicans get elected. I believe our only hope as a nation is to get more qualified, conservative-minded individuals in office to push back against the America-last agenda that is ruining our country.

I attribute my growing respect within the Republican Party to the voters who have supported me. Over and over, the polls show that I am doing the right thing for the American people. Other representatives have started to notice. The voice of the people is important, and, while often forgotten, most of our country lives between the Left Coast and the big city liberals of DC and New York.

Yes, I have called my fellow Republicans to account, but it's not just to attack for no reason. It's to hold all of us accountable to the values that built this country—values from which we've strayed. I have also supported many, and I am glad to bring my voice to aid theirs as they fight for the conservative principles that will save our country. We are the party that will revive America, and I want all of us to be successful.

I believe I have a role to play in continuing to shape the Republican Party into what it must become in order to stand up against corporate interests, globalist policies, and the America-last idiocy that has destroyed our factories, killed our jobs, broken our families, and weakened our country. President Trump proved that we *could* return our lost jobs and investments to the forgotten parts of America and the people Democrats have left behind.

Fighting back against the establishment is not going to be comfortable or easy; we are going to have to push. I knew I would likely not make friends at first, but I've got plenty of friends back home, and they're telling me I'm doing the right thing with their votes and donations.

People must know that the Democrat narrative cannot change the truth. They have to know that we can fight back against the lies, misinformation, and political assassination attempts that the Deep State uses to sabotage any voice that threatens its power. No one is beyond the law; we are all to be treated equally, despite what we've seen in some high-profile cases.

Justice will be served, and the American people will have a voice. That voice will include mine as long as I am here to speak for them— and I won't let the legacy media stand in the way of getting the word out. Let's look at them next, because they are the mouthpiece for the Democrat party, and communicating with the American people is a whole other story when you must also fight the media itself.

5

The Mouthpiece of the Democrat Party

When I first ran for Congress, the Atlanta Journal and Constitution did a profile piece on me. They do articles like this for many new candidates—where you're from, your career, what seat you're running for, and your overall beliefs. It was fair, not bad at all. I'm pretty sure it has been one of the only nice media pieces on me since!

Once you are a declared candidate, the opposition party does their research to see if you're a credible threat, and they quickly built a dossier on me. I wasn't some moderate Republican who would play the game; I was an America-first, MAGA, Christian conservative—and, worst of all, unapologetic about my views. When they saw who I was, they got to work, because, as we've all seen, the legacy media is the mouthpiece of the Democrat party.

I ran for Congress against eight Republican men and won my primary with 40.3 percent of the vote. Candidates must have 50 percent, which meant we would have a runoff.[8] During the runoff, I beat another Republican by over fourteen points, and that called it. With those numbers, no Democrat could win my district. Winning the runoff essentially won me the election, and the Democrat candidate dropped out before the general election was even held.

That's when the firestorm began as the press turned up the heat, knowing I was coming to Washington.

A friend warned me, "Marjorie, when you come to Washington, the legacy media is going to come down like fire from heaven. It's going to be scorching fire on you, and they're going to do everything they can to destroy you."

My friend was wrong—about one thing, anyway. The firestorm started before I even arrived in Washington, DC!

The mainstream media is very powerful, and they do the Democrat's dirty work by shaping people's opinions. They try to control the narrative by covering (or failing to cover) specific events or covering the material in a biased or even misleading way. They deliberately label people, creating a caricature of someone that is entirely false. This is what they did to me.

The media decided to paint me as a racist, conspiracy-theory-believing homophobe—not to mention antisemitic, Islamophobic, and whatever other words they could look up from the Left's playbook of common lies. Once they labeled me as a hate-filled bigot, they made sure to include those labels *every time* my name was mentioned. I was always introduced in pieces with labels such as, "Far-right conspiracy theorist Marjorie Taylor Greene. . . ." I never saw my name in legacy media without a list of labels surrounding it. This was done so their audience wouldn't forget exactly who they'd painted me to be, and it served to sway opinions.

The labels they put on me were for a character that doesn't exist. I am not who they say I am.

The press has learned that if they can destroy you in the court of public opinion, where you don't need facts to get a "conviction," they can beat you by ruining your reputation, potentially even ending your career before it's begun. Powerful corporate media companies will use their shows, social media, and articles to assassinate your character. They lie, misrepresent, and fabricate whatever they want, often without repercussions, as they control the narrative.

But I'm different from most politicians in a significant way: I didn't come to Washington for a career or to make friends or gain influence. I wasn't there for superficial reasons. I came to Washington to change the Republican party and save this country by *doing my job.*

Unlike so many others taken out by the press, their attacks didn't stick. My family, friends, and district knew the truth, and the attacks rolled off my back. The amount of effort they put into attacking me told me something: I was over the target, and I was a threat to them!

Few conservatives have had the strength to punch back against the media. President Trump did it regularly, but I was determined to hit back against their lies. After filing articles of impeachment on Joe Biden and getting kicked off my committees, I called them out on the lies they sold to the American people every day. I declared that, although they had labeled me a conspiracy theorist, *they* were the real conspiracy theorists. I went on to explain that CNN was no different than QAnon, and that the story they tried to sell about Russian collusion was a lie they'd spread far and wide., I began calling them "legacy media conspiracy theorists" to their faces. I like that term better than "fake news" because "conspiracy theorist" is what they hit me with. They spin tales and sell lies on their powerful platforms, swaying the opinions of voters to help achieve the Democrat party's goals and fundraising efforts.

I punched right back by exposing their lies!

Journalism was once a great art and respected trade. Tragically, there are very few real journalists today., Our Founding Fathers gave us a tremendous gift when they wrote in freedom of the press as an American right. Yet our ability to use the freedom of the press to hold our government accountable has been stripped away. Political activists and intelligence agents posing as journalists use the power of the pen to hide under the protection of a free press while destroying America.

Most members of Congress are terrified of the media; if they get a bad news story, they go into panic mode. The media's articles have caused people to change statements, their position on a topic or bill, and even their votes. I'm not like that; I don't care what the media has to say. They lie about people all the time—just look at all the false information they spread about President Trump from the moment he became the Republican nominee for president in 2016. Not to mention the salacious lies they have spread about me!

If they didn't know it already, Republican voters learned they couldn't trust the legacy media and their coverage of President Trump. As a result, conservatives across the nation, including every-one in my district, understood what "fake news" was, giving me an advantage. By calling them out on their lies, President Trump paved the way to fight back against the fabricated media narrative of con-spiracy theories. The press has an agenda; you cannot believe what you hear on the nightly news because it's not the news; it's just their "story." Their "truth" is really the talking points laid out by the Deep State and the Democrat party. That is why they all say the same words and messaging on any given topic. The Washington Press Club and media editors send the same 4:00 a.m. talking points and questions, and like obedient little soldiers, they type, say, and spin the tales that make headlines.

Had I not learned from President Trump how to handle the media attacks, I, too, could've been destroyed. But he showed us the model for taking on the press—and winning! By the time I ran, people understood that if the press attacked and called me names, I was doing something right, and they would like me. The louder the media says something, the less believable it is. We now check to see how they're misrepresenting people and facts.

As people investigated the various media lies and found out what I *really said*, they found they agreed with me! Oddly, it's turned out to be a blessing that the legacy media so clearly tipped their hand (and lies) with President Trump. Now we all know we cannot take reporting at face value but must learn the facts ourselves.

But being attacked and torn apart, even when it's by liars, hurts. I've been called every name in their book, and they've gone after my family, friends, employees, and even my neighbors! The press tries to grill them frequently. "Do you agree with her statements?" they'll ask. Or, "How do you feel about her being a racist?" They ask horrible trick questions, but everyone who knows me has turned against them. Whenever these so-called reporters reached out, my people would refuse to talk to them, and now they hate the press.

In the face of these attacks, my friends and family have bonded and drawn closer together. While they protect me from libel and slander, they also need to protect themselves. Given the chance, the legacy media would print their names and their relation to me while twisting their words and using them to lie about me some more. A few of my friends found out—the hard way—that the legacy media would smear them in their stories and never print or show their full statements. Now they don't trust the media, and they refuse to have anything to do with them, and I don't blame them one bit. I don't think anyone trusts the legacy media anymore, either.

Mom Didn't Raise a Racist

One of the most common lies is that I'm a racist. When the media started using this tired old lie, which they try with every conservative, it really upset my mom, who helped set the record straight. My mom responded that it was ridiculous and went on to explain, "A Black minister baptized you when you were a baby. Growing up, every day, you played with a little Vietnamese girl who flew out on one of the last orphan planes from Vietnam and was adopted into a loving family. Your two other best friends were Korean, a brother and sister. You played with two brothers across the street, who were Black, and a Jewish girl from down the street. They were your best friends, and you had more minority kids than white kids in your group." She went on to point out that my ex-husband and I vacationed with our best friends and their kids, who were African-American and lived across the street. We loved that family dearly and helped raise their girls just as they helped raise our kids.

My entire life, I have never judged people or chosen friends based on their skin color or identity. I like people for who they are, not what they look like. The media wasn't operating on proof when they called me a racist; they rarely do. It's a tired old trope and a default tactic with them.

They called me antisemitic because I attacked George Soros, who happens to be Jewish. The attacks I've made on Soros are because he's destroying democracy with his politics, not because of his ethnicity or religion. Never mind that nobody has called the Left antisemitic for their relentless attacks on Sheldon Adelson and his family.

They like to say that conservatives are fascists, but have you ever seen such blatant, power-crazed government overreach as these blue states' and cities' response during the COVID pandemic? My criticism of Soros or, during the pandemic, vaccine passports was not antisemitic because it has nothing to do with the people of Israel or Judaism. My criticism is about the policies of Soros and against the actual fascist behavior of the Democrat communists forcing segregation of the vaccinated and unvaccinated.

My voting record reflects my true beliefs and sentiments. I've always voted to stand with Israel; we have voted to fund the country. I am one of Israel's biggest defenders in the House, and I have openly fought the Squad over their support of Hamas, Hezbollah, and Palestinian terrorism against Israel. They're the real anti-Semites, but you'll never hear the media say that about them, despite their antisemitic statements and voting records. Take Rashida Tlaib's comments at an American Muslims for Palestine event where she proudly proclaimed "you cannot claim to hold progressive values yet back Israel's apartheid government."[9]

The media also likes to label me homophobic because I advocate for the Protect Children's Innocence Act, which is my legacy bill. I'll share more details later, but for now, understand it's the most important piece of legislation I've ever introduced and may ever introduce in my lifetime. This bill makes it a felony for anyone to perform so-called "gender-affirming care" on kids under eighteen; the bill will protect children from harmful puberty blockers, horrible hormone treatments, and genital mutilation surgeries such as mastectomies, hysterectomies, castrations, and so forth. It will also allow the victims of these transitions to sue the people who did this to them once they are old enough to realize what they've done to their bodies and are experiencing the terrible physical consequences of this medical malpractice.

I don't attack people for being gay, and honestly, I don't want to know what consenting adults do sexually with each other, but I definitely oppose the trans agenda with everything in me. They're grooming and sexualizing children, and that's precisely what pedophiles do, pure and simple. This doesn't make me anti-trans or homophobic; it makes me *a protector of* our kids. I am a mother, and that is what good mothers do. We protect our kids from any form of evil or attack. As Christians, we are commanded to protect innocent people from evil, and our children are the most innocent among us.

I'm not attacking anyone's sexuality, but the choices you make as an adult are entirely different from the choices made as a minor. They cannot vote, smoke, drink, or even get a tattoo. I will work to protect our kids at every turn in addition to opposing the attack on women's rights and safety that is trying to put biological men in women's sports, bathrooms, locker rooms, and prisons. Again, this doesn't make me transphobic, but it does mean I am a modern-day feminist, and I will defend women's and girls' rights; after all, I am a woman and a mother of two daughters. Every parent of a little girl should realize that biological males have no business in women's private places.

It's time to call these men who pose as women and sneak into places they don't belong precisely what they are: Predators who are determined to sexually assault women and girls, defeat women, and ultimately replace women. They aren't women, and they're the greatest threat to women's rights and womanhood!

It's incredible how far we have sunk that we must make these kinds of statements, but I believe it will only get worse if we do not stand up to these lies about gender and the assault on women and kids' safety. For example, in the rules of the 117th Congress, which Nancy Pelosi introduced and Democrats voted to pass, we weren't allowed to use words like male or female, man or woman, boy or girl, or family names like mother, father, brother, sister, aunt, uncle, grandmother, grandfather because those words are offensive to Democrats.[10] When Democrats are in charge, they literally make lies about gender the rules of Congress!

I do not oppose LGB people; I oppose what this tiny special interest group does to everyone else and the danger it poses to vulnerable groups. And I oppose the way the Democrats have embraced the destructive policies that are attacking our kids and women. That's the truth.

Do Your Homework

They like calling me a conspiracy theorist, not just in regards to the idiotic Jewish space laser hit piece and fallout, but also in connection to school shootings. School shootings are real and horrific; they're a testimony to our schools' vulnerability as soft targets and a terrifying, deadly reminder of the depths of what evil and mental illness can lead to. We must work to understand and solve the core problem that causes a person to shoot innocent schoolchildren, teachers, and administrators.

The legacy media pundits didn't do their homework or know my story, but then again, maybe they did. In 1990, after then-Senator Joe Biden had helped make schools gun-free zones, and thus easy targets,[11] I was in a small graduating class of approximately 120 people in Forsyth County, Georgia. I was used to seeing guys at my school with their hunting rifles in the backs of their trucks, and it was common for principals to keep guns in their offices. Most school administrators may have had a gun for safety until Biden and other Democrats took that protection away.

On September 6, 1990, one of the kids attending my school rode the bus and brought three guns to school in a duffle bag. No one thought to check the bag for guns because these shootings weren't happening yet. The student was mad at two other boys who had bullied him, and he planned to kill them that day.

During first period, he pulled out his first gun and tried to take over the classroom! One of the coaches was there and reacted bravely, tackling him to the ground and knocking the gun away. As they fought back and forth, the student was able to pull a second gun from his bag. He fired the weapon and took control of the classroom and the school. We were all held hostage as he threatened to kill everyone there if anyone left.

The only person with a gun that day at my school was a mentally ill, angry, bullied, troubled teenager who was intent on taking at least two lives.

My class was down the hall from the room this boy took hostage, and we learned the terrifying news from teachers. We didn't have cell phones, and we couldn't call for help or search for news. We sat in fear, wondering, "What if he comes down here?" Our windows didn't open wide enough to escape, there was no campus officer, and the principal no longer had his gun. What would we do, hide in the closet? Our lives were held at the whim of a mentally disturbed boy for five grueling hours while we feared for our lives and listened to helicopters circle overhead.

I could see police officers and others running by the windows, and we knew they had the school surrounded, but no one could stop him without putting everyone at risk. There was no good guy with a gun or any type of security to prevent illegal guns from being brought into our school.

At sixteen, I discovered what it was like to be a victim of so-called gun violence in schools. I learned that day that I never wanted to be at the mercy of a bad guy with a gun while good guys were prevented from carrying guns. I realized that we have a Second Amendment right to protect ourselves, and others, with our guns. This is particularly important when the Democrats want to take that safety away by removing the guns that protect our kids from our schools.

I also learned that day that every child, teacher, and person in our schools deserve the same protection we give our politicians and banks. Our children are our most precious resource—they're the future! We owe it to each child to protect them at least as well as we do our money in the banks or precious gold, silver, and jewels! Yet the very people who want to take guns out of the hands of the good guys' are the ones who hire private security, enjoying the taxpayer-funded protection of good guys with guns such as our Capitol Police and Secret Service. Just look at hypocritical politicians like Joe Biden and Nancy Pelosi with their security teams. You can see how much they enjoy the protection of armed guards with rifles while they work to remove AR-15s from private citizens, refuse to harden schools, and demand that schools remain dangerously soft targets by staying gun-free zones.

We were lucky that day in high school—they were able to talk our disturbed schoolmate out of killing anyone. After five hours, his medication had begun to take effect, and the side effects made him sleepy. Thankfully, he was so tired that the authorities were able to convince him to put his guns down and give up. No one died, thank God!

My dad was the first person I saw as I finally left the school, and I'll never forget how scared he looked. We locked eyes, I ran to him, and he hugged me tightly. There are no words for the relief I felt at finally being *safe in his embrace.*

I have carried that experience with me every day since. As a mother, I worried daily about my own children's safety while they were growing up attending gun-free schools. I prayed it wouldn't happen to them and mourned for the families affected by every horrific school shooting America saw on the news.

I'm passionate about defending our Second Amendment rights and our kids. Before I ever thought of running for Congress, I visited Washington several times to lobby as a citizen, asking members of Congress to protect our gun rights—and our kids. I would eventually campaign on this point, telling my personal story from the eleventh grade.

As I went before Congress, frequently as a lone citizen lobbyist, I faced *huge* money groups like Moms Demand Action, March for Our Lives, and Every Town for Gun Safety, Michael Bloomberg's big group that he established in 2014 with a 50-million-dollar pledge.[12] He has reportedly donated over $270 million to causes and candidates pursuing strict gun control laws.[13]

Many of these groups have a seemingly never-ending supply of money donated by wealthy millionaires and billionaires. They enjoy security with guns and their children attend fancy private schools, which are rarely at risk of random school shootings, unlike the gun-free public schools all our kids attend. The gun-grabbing activists come to Washington with every resource, from lawyers to handlers, and even have the matching t-shirts you'd expect from a group-think-controlled political action regiment. They swarm Capitol Hill in large groups as they lobby representatives' and senators' offices, while holding ongoing demonstrations and press conferences. The media eat them up, giving them free coverage, and rightfully so. I've never seen the NRA, or any other pro-Second Amendment group, organize large groups of their members to do citizen lobbying and activism on Capitol Hill.

I've interacted with many of these groups, first as a citizen and Second Amendment activist and now as a representative. This is where I met David Hogg, a former student from Parkland High School, the scene of a horrific school shooting. The lie from the media is that I attacked him; I didn't attack him. Instead, I walked next to him while asking him some tough questions, and it was all on video. By this time, David was out of high school, over eighteen, and being used as a tool of the most powerful gun-grabbing groups. It's interesting we could have such different reactions to our close calls with school shootings, but I shouldn't have been surprised, given his political family. They groomed him to be an activist and actor for the Left immediately after the Parkland shooting. Ever since then, he's made a financially rewarding career for himself being a paid spokesman and prolific fundraiser.

We could have learned from early situations like the one at my school. I wonder how many kids have died because they took the guns that protect our kids from the people who could keep them safe and turned our schools into killing fields by making them gun-free zones. We need to repeal the Gun-Free School Zone Act, putting the decision on how to protect students back in the hands of states and schools.

I've seen many excellent proposals for keeping our kids safe. It is vital to harden schools and limit access only to those allowed there. Funding a TSA-style security system would be immensely expensive, but other options, such as retired police officers and veterans serving as armed volunteers, would be a fantastic idea. Additionally, we could train teachers and staff members who are willing to carry while working with local law enforcement to provide school resource officers for districts to hire. There are many possibilities, and many schools have done their best to create security systems to prevent school shootings.

Research shows that the best way to stop a bad guy with a gun is a good guy with a gun,[14] but right now, the crazy people of America know that if they go to a school to murder children, schools are soft, easy targets. The twenty-eight-year-old woman (who identified as a man) who shot up the school in Nashville knew there would be no guards. Probably influenced by the medications and hormones she was taking to transition, she saw an opportunity to strike where she could do some real damage.

As a matter of fact, according to her diary, she kept a detailed account of all her plans and training to kill innocent children at a Christian school. Her diary told a disturbing story of how she believed the boy inside her would come out when she went to heaven. None of us will ever comprehend why she believed she must murder innocent people and little children in order to go to heaven and turn into a boy. If you understand God, it just doesn't work that way. As a matter of fact, that is how Satan works; he deceives the minds of the weak and broken and convinces them to commit all kinds of sins, even the unthinkable—killing innocent little children—and that leads directly to the path of eternal damnation, not heaven.

If we don't protect our schools and look at why people decide to become mass murderers, we're going to have a hard time stopping these shootings. In the case of the Nashville shooter, she was on medications and hormones. One study showed that between 1900 and 2017, 59 percent of shooters were people diagnosed with mental health issues or had acted in threatening ways before the shootings.[15] People struggling with their mental health are not inherently dangerous, but we must look at the connections behind these shooters and the role of medications like SSRIs and other treatments.

We should've learned a lesson the day my school was held hostage by a would-be school shooter, but Joe Biden, and other politicians in Washington, DC, refused to learn that lesson. Instead, they continued with their gun-free school zones, and they ensured it was signed into law. This left children all over the country vulnerable to dangerous individuals with psychological problems, convinced that an evil act of murder could somehow deliver the result they were looking for. We must make our schools safe instead of mindlessly swallowing the media's narrative as they try to pin gun violence on white men and legal gun owners.

Hand-in-Glove

I could spend an entire chapter just talking about the various lies the media has told about me, but I think you get the idea. So instead, let's look at how the media's influence directly benefits the Democrat party. The media coverage of conservatives like President Trump and I aren't just political hit pieces; these awful stories are a gift on a platter to the Democrats, both in coverage and in funding.

When the media runs their hack stories, it helps groups like the Southern Poverty Law Center (SPLC) make money from their famous slogan, "Make hate pay." For instance, let's say the legacy media writes a horrible story about me. The Democrat consultants in the Democratic Congressional Campaign Committee (DCCC) use these lying news stories to write fundraising emails, newsletters, social media posts, and calls to their political action committees

(PACs). They use the fake image they create of me as a racist, anti-semitic, homophobic conservative to scare Democrat voters into donating money.

This makes the legacy media not just the mouthpiece for the Democrat party but also their fundraisers! They lie about me, slander me, mischaracterize me, and then sell this load of crap to the American people (at least the ones who still watch them). Next, when the DCCC and other fundraisers call, these misinformed and frightened people donate to Democrats they think will "stand up" to me. It's not hard to demonize me in the fundraiser because the media already used all their labels to mischaracterize and attack me every time my name is mentioned.

They tried to do this in my district during my 2022 primary election when I ran against Marcus Flowers, a Democrat and Black veteran. I easily won, but he ran on every hate label the media had used to portray me, calling me a racist, homophobic, antisemitic, hateful person—he just used the media's lies repeatedly in his campaign. He raised around $15 million with this technique,[16] but he couldn't win even then! While it didn't work against me, imagine this same story played out in election after election across our country.

The legacy media, with its salacious lies, is a big help to the Democrat party; their never-ending stream of hit pieces against me should be registered as in-kind donations to all the various Democrat political arms and candidates because of all their defamatory stories. And the same should especially apply to President Trump!

I recently had the opportunity to appear on 60 Minutes, the longest-running news magazine program in American history. Leslie Stahl, a trailblazer for women in journalism, media, and television for nearly fifty years, did the interview. Love her or hate her, she's had an amazing career.

I wasn't going to do it initially, but my communications director Nick Dyer talked me into it. They recorded hours and hours of footage as Leslie asked me many questions as they accompanied me to my office, hometown, restaurants, and even a GOP event. Then, they cut it down to a thirteen-minute segment of an hour-long program, beginning with Leslie calling me all the nasty names the Left and their friends in the media have been calling me.

"Looks like a typical troll in my Twitter feed," I responded to Leslie. "I just don't care. I don't let name-calling bother me or offend me." Ironically, she later told *me* that I needed to stop calling people names, which made me laugh at her hypocrisy.

Her biggest complaint? I call Democrats pedophiles for sexualizing children. Yet, that's *exactly* what pedophiles do—and that's why my Protect Children's Innocence Act is so vital. Leslie laughed at me, which tells me they don't get it. They don't understand that sexualizing minors is wrong.

The 60 Minutes crew did a decent job reporting about my childhood and career before I entered politics. They showed me working out and going about life, but there was so much they didn't show. For example, Leslie and I actually got *along*. She apparently liked me, and many of her questions were pleasant, but they didn't show much of that. I was just grateful that I held my own even in the significantly cut and edited thirteen-minute piece they aired.

After the interview, I found it fascinating how people came out to support me, but it was also interesting to see who had a problem with it. Franklin Graham's support was a big compliment—and he was attacked for saying something nice about me.[17] They attacked Leslie Stahl for interviewing me;[18] I think the unstated rule of the Left is not to give me a platform where I can debunk their deceptions but instead just misquote and lie to get their headlines.

The women on *The View*, of course, attacked me in their typically nasty fashion almost weekly. I find it funny that the people who come up to me and say the most hateful things are usually white women, maybe ten years older than I am, typically still wearing a mask and sometimes towing a neatly dressed husband behind them. They'll come up to me in airports or restaurants, usually in DC, and tell me I'm a horrible person. They'll call me horrible names. I always ask them, "You watch *The View*, right?" Sure enough, they pretty much all do. Some of the most hateful people in America are "educated" fifty- to sixty-year-old affluent white women, bored enough to watch *The View* and be spoon-fed filth by nasty women every day.

Bright Spots

I don't want to make it seem like everyone in the media is terrible. While Fox News overall hasn't been a positive experience for me for the most part, I've enjoyed going on Tucker Carlson, who had me on Fox Nation and *Tucker Carlson Tonight*. While Fox has not wanted much to do with me, which I've never understood, Tucker and a few others have cared enough to get their information on me straight. Unfortunately, even though Tucker Carlson was number one, not just on Fox News but out of everyone, Fox News fired him. We all know Tucker will be back, probably by the time this book is out.

I have heard, but it's not verified, that I'm on a blacklist with Fox News (other than a few opinion shows), which is the exact opposite of journalism. No media company should be in the business of censorship, but if a company has a member of Congress blacklisted, then that's exactly what they're engaging in—censorship.

Not only did they fire the number one host of their company in all primetime shows, but they also canceled Don Jr. After not having him on air for a year, they asked Don to appear and talk about his father's indictment the day it happened. They canceled on Don five minutes before his segment. Apparently, they had someone more qualified to speak about his father's indictment.

In spite of all that, they all talk *about* me. Imagine if they just talked *to* me.

Podcasts and radio shows have been better, and I have been on Real America's Voice, Charlie Kirk, Alex Jones, Donald Trump Jr., OANN, Newsmax, and others. But I would appear on more news shows as well, and maybe, one day, I will.

I see everybody who works in the Capitol media frequently, and, honestly, I've seen them work hard. I have a lot of respect for hard work. I just wish many of them would put their hard work into real journalism instead of political activism or be brave enough to stand up to their communist editors and ditch the Press Club's talking points. Even though they attack me, I will fight for their First Amendment rights, because if we don't have freedom of the press and free speech, we've exchanged our representative democracy for totalitarian communism. This is honestly happening far too much in our country; just look at the Left's attempts at censoring whatever they deem "misinformation."

Even when I don't agree with someone, I can appreciate those who work hard. Into my second year of Congress, I saw how hard some reporters work—sometimes physically running to catch up and talk to someone, asking questions on the fly while recording. And sometimes, they will literally run to the next interview! I'm not sure if they need to spend more time in the gym to squeeze in their workouts or if their jobs give them all the workouts they need!

I'm not vindictive, and I do not hold grudges, so I began appreciating some of the media members' hard work and their ability to dig for that next story. I am nice to them, and I try to take time to stop and answer their questions. I can say that things have become slightly nicer between some press members and me. I think maybe a few have even begun to respect me!

It probably began when I gained real power and influence within my Republican conference. Perhaps they realized that they hadn't killed my political career like they'd set out to do, and the reality was I was gaining influence and beginning to move the needle. It was forcing my party to change around *me*, rather than DC changing me, that made me newsworthy.

Or perhaps it was doing a bus tour in my district with the press at the recommendation of Nick Dyer. I was mad at him (again) and didn't want to do it. "Take them with you the whole day," he suggested. "Allow them to follow you around, talk to everybody you talk to, and see you at home in your district—and how people treat you. I want them to see you as a real person."

I came *unglued* at Nick! He wanted me to spend an entire *day* with those who treated me poorly. How could he ask this?

He persisted, I finally agreed, and he set it up.

My mom always taught me to put my best foot forward, so I decided I would give it a try—one time. After all, what more could they say and lie about that was any worse than they'd already done? The least I could do was go about the day, being myself at home in my district, with the people I love.

So, I got on a bus with many media members, several who hated me and said horrible things about me. I ate with them, met people with them, and talked with them. And I did it with a good attitude! I wanted to see them as real people, and I wanted them to see me the same way.

I decided that, even if they treated me like garbage, I would just be myself around them. I was honest and unabashedly myself the whole day. I tried to be sincere, and I still talked about everything I would've usually spoken about if they weren't there. But I also dared to be transparent and authentic with them.

And do you know what? It went pretty well until this guy, Rick Folbaum from Channel 9 WANF in Atlanta, decided to be that fake news jerk the rest of them had always been. We were at a stop, and I had just voted for myself in the primary before returning to do a press conference with the media members of the bus tour. He turned his microphone on, the camera was rolling, and he began accusing me of all the stupid common lies they tell about me. He immediately charged me with things like being a QAnon conspiracy theorist, leading the insurrection on January 6, and all the rest of their tired old crap.

I *unloaded* on this guy! I chewed him out quite effectively, and the people in the crowd began to cheer and chew him out, too. I wasn't going to take it anymore; I had been nice to him all day, showing my authentic self and letting them see a solid glimpse into my life. They had met the people of my district, who are good, hard-working Americans. And here, right in front of my supporters, he dared to treat me like that? I simply wouldn't take it! But I'll be honest; it felt pretty good to give it right back to him.

I could tell the impact of having the press along. Even though they still might not like me, they spent time with me, got to see my district, met the good people who live here, and saw the incredible support that I have. After spending nearly two years attacking and lying about me in their news stories, perhaps they learned I'm not the monster and character they created in their stories. Their lies didn't damage me a single bit or convince any of the voters in my district of any conspiracy theories about me. In fact, the media just continued to discredit themselves with their vicious name-calling and lying attacks.

More importantly, whether they like it or not, the media needs to understand that I represent the views of many Americans. It was wrong when Hillary Clinton labeled us all "deplorables." We make up roughly half of the nation, and the Democrats and the media cast us all aside like we no longer mattered. I hope the media realizes that when they treat me poorly with baseless name-calling, it makes those who voted for me and support me feel as if the media is treating them that way, too.

I have told them to their faces multiple times that, despite the terrible things they have said and the names they have called me, I am one of the only members of Congress who would defend their rights and the freedom of the press to say those things. Unlike Democrats, like Joe Biden, I will protect that constitutional right because it preserves the First Amendment, which Joe Biden and the Democrats want to demolish to stop the spread of supposed disinformation, misinformation, and anything else that doesn't align with their twisted narrative. Whether the Left admits it or not, that is an Orwellian tactic, and the members of the media should be genuinely afraid that one day, Joe Biden or some other Democrat administration's misinformation police will come after them for saying the wrong thing.

Fight for Freedom

I'm in Washington to do a job—and that job even involves fighting for freedom of the press for those who say the most hateful things about me. I will protect their voices, even if they don't like me, tell lies about me, call me names, and say the most horrible things about me.

One of the most disappointing and frustrating things is that the press spends most of their time reporting the weaponized government attacks on President Trump while entirely ignoring the actual crimes committed by Joe Biden and his family. Joe Biden has classified documents irresponsibly stored everywhere, from Chinatown in Washington, DC, to his garage floor next to his Corvette.[19] Yet, President Trump is charged with thirty-seven absurd charges, ignoring the Presidential Records Act, which allows former presidents to possess classified information. Everyone is so sick of the hypocrisy!

While they froth at the mouth on MSNBC about all things Trump, they completely ignore actual facts revealed through a whistleblower and an unclassified 1023 form that proves that Joe Biden took a $5 million bribe while he was Vice President of the United States to get Viktor Shokin, the Ukrainian prosecutor, fired when he was going after Burisma, the oil and gas company on which Hunter Biden sat on the board.[20]

I know all of this to be true because I serve on the Oversight Committee and was forced to read the redacted unclassified 1023 form in a SCIF by Joe Biden lackey, FBI Director Christopher Wray. And one of the redacted parts said there were seventeen audio recordings of Hunter and Joe Biden! That alone should infuriate a free press—the FBI Director protected his boss, the president, and refused to comply with our Oversight Committee subpoena! Instead, one quick story and back to Trump, Trump, Trump!

Imagine our country if the legacy press told that story as much as they regurgitated the Trump attack conspiracy theories? We would be a different country and perhaps kinder towards one another.

Despite everything, I don't call the legacy press "fake news" that much anymore, as strange as that may seem to many conservatives. Many media members, who have met with me face-to-face and got to know me a little, have stopped their baseless attacks, but not all of them. I always hope for the best in people and that those working in the media will return to trustworthy journalism. I hope they remember how precious our free press is and that its purpose, from our Founding Fathers, is to tell the American people the truth about what happens in our government, without political bias, so the American people can hold their government accountable.

We should never forget Eric Snowden, a whistleblower who released classified information from the NSA that exposed the US Intelligence spying capabilities and their ability to spy on everyone about everything. Snowden revealed no one's communication was private, and it still isn't.

The most remarkable example of freedom of the press and the need for government transparency is Julian Assange, who released sensitive and confidential information that exposed many sins of our US government. The information released included 57,000 messages from the Pentagon, FBI, FEMA, and New York Police officials. Assange claimed these messages showed a nuanced understanding of how the tragic events on 9/11 that killed over three thousand Americans led us into a nearly twenty-year war in the Middle East. Assange also released a video by then-Army soldier Bradley Manning showing US Apache helicopter attacks in Baghdad that killed at least nine men, including a Reuters news photographer and his driver. It's odd that today, Julian Assange is jailed, facing prosecution by the US and other countries, while Bradley Manning (now a transgender "woman" named Chelsea Manning) lives a free life here in the United States, even though Manning is the one who gave Julian Assange the video.

Assange shared information that shocked the world about America. In the famous WikiLeaks file, Assange released documents on Iraq and Afghanistan detailing civilian deaths, the hunt for Osama bin Laden, and Iran's backing of militants in Iraq, in addition to over 250,000 diplomatic cables from the State Department, dating from 1966 to 2010, revealing all kinds of classified information about the US, now known as Cablegate.

It's hard to understand how Assange can release Cablegate, yet our government still won't release the John F. Kennedy assassination files,[21] and the FDA hid Pfizer vaccine safety data for seventy-five years until a judge ordered it released.[22] This is definitely a fight for the truth.

As alarming as the Cablegate revelations were, the leak that likely did Assange in was the release of nearly 20,000 Democratic National Committee emails and another two thousand emails from Hillary Clinton's campaign manager, John Podesta. Among many insights, like how the Democrat presidential primary was stolen from Bernie Sanders, the emails also told how DNC Chairwoman Donna Brazile had given the Clinton campaign debate questions in advance. When it comes to elections, never forget: Democrats cheat.

Ahh, but Russia, Russia, Russia!

Tucker Carlson is the most recent person punished for pushing too hard against the Deep State or the legacy mega-media company Fox News. With journalism that's rarely seen and in brave fashion, Tucker used his nightly primetime show to tell the American peo-ple, and arguably the world, the truth about every topic. He cov-ered woke corporate policies like ESG, dared to talk about voting machine companies, absentee ballots, and stolen elections, and told the truth about how America had no business funding and waging a proxy war with nuclear-armed Russia in Ukraine. To the shock and anger of the establishment in Washington, DC, Americans agreed with Tucker Carlson. Tucker told the truth too much. His coverage was destroying the stale old messaging tactics and decades-old PSYOP (*psychological operations*) tactics deployed against Americans by the Deep State. It's the Deep State that really runs Washington and the legacy media.

No company fires someone like Tucker Carlson. He was raking in obscene amounts of ad dollars night after night while consistently maintaining a massive lead as the number-one show on cable news.

Tucker Carlson was also one of the only people in the legacy media who would interview me, allowing me to share the work I was doing in Congress and tell my side. Never attacking, he let me tell the truth, which I appreciated more than he could know.

Tucker now does his show on X, formerly Twitter, his content garnering between 30 million and 250 million views on each post. These numbers are proof that Tucker's thoughts are precisely how Americans think and feel, not the way the legacy media tells them to think and feel.

The right to a free press is one of the most amazing things about our country. I genuinely hope that one day more brave people inside the legacy media will use their right of a free press to inform the people about our corrupt government. Still, I'm sure the fate of Julian Assange and Tucker Carlson stand as glaring reminders not to stray from the 4 a.m. talking points.

One of the beautiful things about our country is that, even though we may not agree with everyone, we recognize they have the right to say their piece. Our right to freedom of speech is precious, and we should be upset about the attacks the Democrats have made on these freedoms, ironically, in the name of preserving democracy.

And I will do my job to protect that right.

After all, Alex Jones was right about one thing: It really is an information war, and the truth is worth fighting for.

6

The Real Racists

One of the oldest plays in the book of both Democrats and their buddies in the media is the racism card. When objecting to a Republican, if they don't have anything of substance to say, they just default to calling us racists. The reality is that the Democrat party's focus on identity politics shows that they are the racist ones; they use race, gender, and a host of other labels to divide America. They put value on someone's identity politics, not based on their character, competence, or merit.

There's a word for people who do that: racist!

I'm tired of watching the Democrat party blatantly use people and groups as leverage to gain more power and then fail to benefit those people. They talk such great talk about protecting minorities. Still, no one did more for minority unemployment than President Trump, who was called a racist constantly by the legacy media and the Democrats.

Everything is "racist" for the Democrats. In Georgia, you're required to have an identification card or Social Security number to receive government assistance like welfare or PeachCare. You must show your ID to get assistance, yet Stacey Abrams and others have tried to fight what they call Jim Crow voting laws—namely, that you have a valid ID. So, they claim that voter ID is racist and suppresses the vote. Yet most states have requirements, just like Georgia, and no one complains that those are racist. To me, it's the opposite; Abrams' argument is insulting to Black Americans' intelligence, insinuating that Black voters aren't capable of getting an ID card, which is ridiculous.

This is par for the course and shows how much the Democrats look down on minority groups like African Americans. They see them as tools and insult their intelligence regularly. To me, it's a slap in the face and should show the whole country that Democrats are a racist group who use skin color to achieve their goals.

The Racism of Identity Politics

Identity politics take away from individuals and attempt to categorize everyone. By destroying the individuality of a person, you take away their freedom. The Democrats have gotten very good at turning people into mindless herds of sheep that they can control. These good little followers won't ask questions or think critically because they like the government taking care of them, even though the government does a horrible job of taking care of them.

The Democrats want to turn us into a communist nation where the government takes care of people and controls everything, where the government is God, maintaining your standard of life and meeting all your needs. That is *not* America—we believe in God, and we believe that the people have the power, not the government!

The Democrats' identity politics is insulting. I listen to Vice President Kamala Harris, who was selected because she's a minority woman of color. Depending on where she is, sometimes she's Indian, and sometimes she's Black. She was educated in Canada, but if she's speaking to a mostly Black audience, she puts on this affected accent like she was raised in a Black community in the South. How insulting is that? The only thing worse is when Hillary Clinton does it!

It astounded me when Joe Biden picked Pete Buttigieg for Secretary of Transportation because he knows *nothing* about transportation! He's as unqualified for that post as Hunter Biden was to work for a Ukrainian oil and gas company. Yet because he's a married gay man with adopted children, he portrays another group Democrats seek to use.

And don't get me started on Admiral Rachel Levine, formerly Richard Levine, who is now the assistant secretary for health. Previously, Levine was a doctor in Pennsylvania who mandated that senior COVID patients be put back in their nursing homes . . . while taking *his* mother out to live in a hotel! The first transgender admiral (not because of service in our Navy but in the US Public Health Service Commissioned Corps), Levine's policy led to 12,500 nursing home deaths, accounting for a sickeningly high percent of Pennsylvania's COVID deaths.[23] The incompetent decision is bad; taking his mom out right before issuing the policy is terrible! Now this failure is in charge of our government's pediatric decisions, including transitioning, puberty blockers, and hormones, which he believes are the right treatments for children with gender dysphoria.

I believe in hiring qualified people of high character. But Joe Biden and the Democrats have demonstrated that your sexual preferences and identification mean infinitely more to them than your abilities or record.

A Big Lie

The funny thing is that when people today talk about the parties and racism, they are inclined to go with the Democrat narrative (spread by the legacy media) that Republicans are the racist ones. The problem is that the record doesn't back that up. Stretching back to 1829, the Democrat party was on the side of slavery in the Civil War; they were involved with the KKK and its founding; they were the party of segregation (just do a little research into Joe Biden's segregation voting record); and they opposed civil rights. They've been on the wrong side of every issue of identity in politics, and nothing has changed.[24]

The Republicans were the party that freed the slaves when Republicans in Congress voted for freedom.[25] Democrats treated slaves as property, including within the Supreme Court, and it took a civil war to gain their freedom.[26] Just go ahead and look at the party lines of the Supreme Court at that time!

Identity politics is the greatest manipulation and marketing tool in modern-day politics because it's a completely hollow package they can sell. Democrats want to put you in a category and then claim they identify with your issues. But once they have you under their thumb, what are they really doing for Americans? They say they're here to help and protect, but they only want control. And control takes away freedom.

In America, we are free. There aren't any slaves here anymore—and there have not been for generations. At least not legal slaves. Democrats use our country's history of slavery to drive a racist wedge into politics, promising free government handouts and always dangling reparations while trying to erase their own party's real history of slavery, the KKK, and racism.

America is not the land of guaranteed outcomes; it's the land of opportunity. If there's enough opportunity for a Black community organizer from Chicago to get elected President *twice*, it doesn't matter what color you are, what gender you are, or whether or not you're born into poverty. You can study, work hard, apply yourself, and succeed.

People want a handout, but those who really want to go to college find a way. They don't just go if they have scholarships; they work their way through. Others join the military to serve our country, and when they get out, they pay for college with the GI Bill. You can even go into the National Guard and be a reservist, and the military will still pay for your college education! And guess what? You can still be successful even if you don't go to college with the age-old trick of hard work.

Success in America was never the result of a handout; it was the result of hard work. The Left has completely forgotten this concept. They want success to be something the liberal elite allocate, in this case, based on the color of your skin or your gender identity. That is not American!

This alphabet soup of labels—the more letters you add, the better—they use to categorize people by their sexual preferences is nothing short of perverse and inappropriate, especially in front of children. Sexuality is a *private* matter, and making it a public identity is wrong. It should never be how someone identifies themselves, except perhaps on their dating app. Sexuality doesn't belong on a school or job application, and we shouldn't be walking around carrying public labels that identify us by the way we like to have sex.

It's gotten so bad that Democrats are sexualizing *children*. Children aren't mature enough to have sex, and we certainly don't need to be trying to force them into sexual identities before they're even legally of age. We call those who sexualize children *pedophiles*. The Left can call it being a "minor-attracted individual" and come up with a flag all they want, but it's still completely wrong and disgusting.

Democrats have been force-feeding kids this label soup for some time, and the number of kids identifying as trans is sharply rising because they're confused. They are so young they can't get tattoos, smoke, or drink, yet the Left wants them to make lifelong gender preference changes *now*, under eighteen. No way! I will fight against sexualizing children to my last breath.

Identity politics is rooted in Marxism and the belief that identifying classes is necessary to understand and combat oppression among minority groups, but this just serves to divide us. The Pledge of Allegiance talks about us being "indivisible" because we come from a belief that all men and women are created equal—by *God*. So, if God created us all the same, why do Democrats seek to divide us?

United we will stand; divided we will fall.

SCOTUS on Trial

The Supreme Court of the United States is currently made up of six justices appointed by conservatives and three appointed by liberals. Thanks to President Trump appointing Brett Kavanaugh and Amy Coney Barrett, we have had one branch of government that has continued holding back the tide through sound judicial decisions. This court does not pander to the Left, and that has them enraged. In the last year or so, we've seen decisions that have frustrated and angered

Democrats, the most notable of which might be the overturning of *Roe v. Wade*, which put abortion decisions back in the hands of the states.

As I write this, the Court has ruled that affirmative action promoting race as a college admission standard rather than merit is unconstitutional.[27] The Left went wild, including Michelle Obama, who I'm quick to point out was First Lady not once but twice when her husband was voted President of the United States. There are racist idiots in the country, but there aren't enough of them to keep a charismatic African-American man from getting elected to our nation's highest office. He wasn't voted in because of affirmative action but elected by this country's vote, which included a high percentage of white voters.

A recent poll from ABC—not known as a bastion of conservatism—showed that 52 percent of Americans approved of the Supreme Court decision not to use race in college admissions.[28] Only 32 percent disapproved, but as a country with a two-time African-American president, we can say that we don't need affirmative action.

TV personality Joy Reid, who got into Harvard because of affirmative action[29], was, of course, upset that it was being taken away. But just ask yourself, what would happen if colleges admitted the kids who had worked the hardest, studied the longest, and done the work to get in rather than students who simply met a quota? It's the equity versus equality debate, and I'm sure it won't go away any time soon.

They Don't Care

The irony is that the Democrats don't actually care about the things they say they care about. If they cared about racial justice, they wouldn't be working to trade with countries that still have slavery. (According to a recent report there are over fifty million slaves in the world today.[30]) They advocated for "the science" during COVID, but they deny the science of sex (there are only two arrangements of sex chromosomes) and refuse to define what a woman is. They say they stand for women's rights, but they welcome biological men into women's sports in unfair and flat-out dangerous ways. Successful athletes like LeBron James posture about racial topics yet don't blink an eye at the injustices in China, a major source of pro basketball revenue.[31]

The hypocrisy is thick, and it sometimes comes out more often than others. While claiming to love our country, people like Cori Bush are quick to criticize the 4th of July. Her tweet read, "I'm sorry, but anyone happily waving American flags right now is either a gleeful white supremacist or is gleefully uninformed."[32] She demanded reparations while griping about our country for things that happened over two hundred years ago. This is the same Cori Bush who voted to send $113 billion to Ukraine,[33] where they have actual Nazis in their army.[34]

Ben and Jerry's, makers of politically charged ice cream, quickly jumped on the bandwagon, demanding we return the stolen land on which the country is built to the indigenous peoples. As one tweet pointed out, they have yet to contact the tribe that owns the land on which their HQ is based to return it. "Do as I say, not as I do," right?

But the biggest hypocrite of them all is the Big Guy, Joe Biden himself. During the 2020 election, Biden told Charlamagne Tha

God's radio audience that if you voted for Trump, then "you ain't Black," in a Southern preacher voice.[35] His record of racist statements and votes stretches back his entire (lengthy) political career.

In 1977, Biden opposed desegregating schools, stating his kids would grow up "in a racial jungle," and coordinated with segregationist senators to oppose school bussing.[36] Ironically, Kamala Harris landed a blow on him during the 2020 presidential debates when she blamed him directly for her negative experiences as a young girl.[37] Yet when offered a chance to be his VP, Harris jumped at the opportunity to join her oppressor.

Biden showed how he really feels about African Americans when he made a braindead statement regarding Barack Obama, calling him "the first mainstream African American who is articulate and bright and clean."[38] He's backed up his beliefs with one idiotic gaffe after another. Still, the legacy media ignores these and other tasteless comments, for example, claiming Latinos reject COVID vaccinations because they're worried about being deported.

What if Donald Trump had said these things? He'd be vilified and attacked from every corner. What if I had said these awful things? I don't even want to imagine. Any conservative would be politically destroyed for any of these comments, but as a Democrat, Biden gets a pass from his party and the media.

But why do Americans give him a pass? It's obvious that the legacy media ignores the Democrats' racism. Discerning American voters must recognize that the supposed party of racial justice and inclusion is seeding divisiveness and disunity with its actions, all while claiming to be enlightened. Their identity politics serve only to label and divide, and if we want a real chance for everyone in America to thrive again, it's time we get the real racists out of office.

7

Protect Children's Innocence

In 2021, THE DEMOCRATS TRIED to bring legislation to the floor called the Equality Act under the guise of fighting racism and discrimination. This disgusting bill would make it law that biological men would be seen as women. Embracing the trans agenda and attacking women's rights, it would allow them to be in our bathrooms, undress in our locker rooms, and ruin our sports, destroying Title IX.[39] The bill would further force all medical providers to perform abortions, calling it "women's healthcare."[40] The so-called Equality Act was one of the worst and most offensive bills I've ever read.

The Democrat party seems intent on destroying women's rights and killing unborn children up to the day of birth—and then making taxpayers foot the bill. This is so ironic to me, as the Democrats try to position themselves as the champions of women's rights. There is nothing equal about the Equality Act attacking women, removing their safe places such as locker rooms, and killing unborn women (and men) before they even have a chance to breathe. Taking away someone's right to life doesn't seem very equal to me at all!

The debate was intense, with Republicans opposing this terrible bill and standing against the negative impact on women and girls nationwide. I was surprised (but not really) that so many supposed champions of women's rights, Democrats like Marie Newman, who was across the hall from my office, would condone a bill that was such an affront to our gender.[41]

I'd never really paid much attention to which representatives were near my office because we hardly ever saw anyone come in or out of the doors. Marie Newman's office had a sign on the door that said nobody could enter because of COVID. The sign had a number on it, so I thought no one was in. But I got to know her, in a way, fighting this Equality Act.

I "met" Marie when she tagged me in a Twitter post. It was a video of her, with her mask on, looking at the nameplate by my office door. The camera panned to her door across the hall and then to her, holding a trans flag. She looked militant and aggressive, planting the trans flag next to the American flag and state flag outside her office. In the matching place I have beside my door, there is a POW flag. She ended the video by clapping her hands together as though she was all done with something. I remember thinking, usually, when you meet your neighbor, you do so in a friendly way—say, with cookies or a cobbler. But my Democrat neighbor was greeting me with an assault on Twitter and an attack on my very gender with her little trans flag. Unbelievable!

I soon learned more about Marie. She had an adult biological son who identified as a woman—about the same age as my daughters, in their twenties.[42] I couldn't help but be disgusted and pissed because she wanted to vote for a bill that would put her biological son in the same bathrooms as my biological daughters.

Women's sports are important to me, and this was personal. One of my daughters was a D1 fast-pitch softball player in college on scholarships. I watched how hard she worked to *earn* her scholarship to play softball against other biological girls and women who had also worked since they were kids in order to play college ball.

My daughter had played since she was four, was a top competitor, and was highly ranked nationally. If she had to compete for a scholarship against biological males, it would be much harder to get a scholarship because of the inherent advantages a male's testosterone levels give in muscle and size. She would also be at risk of being injured by much bigger, more powerful *male* players. My daughter played catcher and sometimes third base. The power and speed with which a male can hit the ball or collide with a catcher in a slide is a whole other league compared to female competitors.

The fact is, there are plenty of girls and women already getting hurt while facing off against biological men. We talk about the equality of the sexes, and I believe that we are all of equal value. But, after puberty, biological men are typically larger and stronger than women of the same age. Again, it's an issue of hormones, and testosterone (which female athletes cannot inject) is a significant factor in giving biological men physical advantages over female athletes. It is indeed a fact that women are physically the weaker sex.

It is not only morally wrong and unfair; it's *dangerous,* both on and off the field. The Democrats want these *men,* who are trying to make themselves feel good by beating smaller females when they couldn't win competitions against other males, to also invade our girls' privacy. The Democrats want men in the women's bathrooms and locker rooms at schools; places that are supposed to be private and safe. Riley Gaines, a former Kentucky swimmer, and others like her are taking up the fight, championing women, and sharing stories of trans women exposing male genitals to girls in locker rooms. We've had eighteen-year-old trans women exposing themselves to middle school-aged girls of fourteen in locker rooms!

Do you know what we call that? *Indecent exposure and sexual assault!*[43] It's a serious crime in any sensible state, punishable as a felony with a potential of fines and up to ten years in prison in some states.[44] Democrats' erroneously named Equality Act would put these men in the same bathrooms, locker rooms, and even *hotel rooms* as real girls.[45] If you want to know how dangerous that is, just research instances of rape and sexual abuse—crimes that are getting downplayed in this trans insanity.

I thank God my daughter was not put in that situation, though a few of her friends were. The more I read about these injustices to women, the madder I get, and it turns out I was to get my chance to fight by taking on this Equality Act.

I didn't start the fight with Marie Newman, but I responded with my own tweet. I had my staff make a nice sign saying, "There are only two genders, male and female." Below that, it read, "Trust the science." I liked this because Democrats tried to position themselves as the party of science during COVID (much of which was false and misleading). To me, it's simple: God created us, male and female, with just two types of sex chromosome pairs. Either you're XX and a woman, or you're XY and a male. While some people are born with chromosomal disorders or with both sex organs, it is very rare. Throughout all of history, there has never been an argument about sex or gender. It has always been simple—male and female.

We had the sign made up in just a few hours, and together with my staff, I made a video just the way Marie had made hers—except

I wasn't wearing a ridiculous mask. In the place of a trans flag, I held my sign, which I then stuck on the wall next to my flags. I ended the video like she had, clapping my hands as though I was done with a task, and then we posted it. I posted a counterattack, making sure I was referring to Marie in a way that respected gender—as "Marie New*person*" rather than New*man*. Let's just say she didn't like the video that much.

The Left-wing media lost its *mind*, and the trans agenda people— same people, mostly—went crazy, condemning me for attacking Marie Newperson's "daughter" (who was a twenty-something-year-old biological male). The condemnation against me was for attacking a "child" as though he were not an adult. Nonstop hate mail, death threats, and horrible phone calls flooded my office!

Marie, of course, didn't get any hate for trying to put biological men in our girls' locker rooms, where these men indecently expose themselves to minors and have even raped some of them. Oh, no, it would be insensitive to write bad stories about Marie for standing up for all those males who want to be treated as females, especially her own adult son.

Is Justice Really Blind?

This was the opening salvo of a war, not just regarding the Democrat's disgusting bill but also for my male/female sign. It was almost immediately vandalized, and each time we'd make a new sign and put it right back up. This happened eight or nine times. Some of the attacks were weird, such as "Free Palestine" written in marker. Another time, someone began printing out and putting up various stickers that wouldn't peel off. Most of the messages were religious hate speech, attacking me for being a Christian, and others were attacks on me as a woman. The vandalism of my property happened over the course of months, and we figured it was the same person.

I reported the vandalism and the serious death threats to the Capitol Police and the sergeant at arms. I kept asking for Capitol Police protection, but since Nancy Pelosi, then-Speaker of the House, had to sign off for members of Congress, my requests were denied. She would never sign off on a security detail for me, even while other women in Congress, like Cori Bush, AOC, and others, got security details when they received threats.

I demanded a camera, which took forever to get installed. After the camera was installed in the hallway, they caught the person on video within a week. We were notified that they'd seen the person and that Capitol Police had arrested him for vandalizing my property. But they refused to tell me who it was and dragged their feet as the case was referred to the Department of Justice. I thought, surely the guy would be fired and thrown out—that's what *should* happen, right? Well, it didn't.

Weeks went by, and they didn't tell us anything. I kept demanding to know the person's identity; after all, I was still getting death threats, and now they *knew* who was vandalizing my property. What if I met this person, unknowingly, in an elevator or hallway? I wouldn't know if this person meant me harm because the authorities were withholding the information.

Finally, I got a call from a female attorney with the DOJ. She told me flatly that they wouldn't be prosecuting because they didn't think they could get a conviction. "Explain to me," I said carefully, "why you can't get a conviction when it's on *video*? It's undeniable, and it's vandalizing my property—an attack on a member of Congress." In fact, they'd actually caught him on video *twice*.

She replied they didn't think they could get a conviction in court. I asked if he'd at least been fired. Nope! I, again, demanded to know his identity. At that point, I just didn't feel safe, and sometimes I was even sleeping in my office. I told her that if they weren't going to keep me safe, I was going to the press and revealing their refusal to prosecute and that the offender hadn't been disciplined in any way. At this point, the DOJ attorney gave in and said she'd get me the person's name.

When I found out who'd been defacing my property, I was astounded to learn it was Tim Hysom, the chief of staff to Democrat Congressman Jake Auchincloss! I couldn't believe it; I expected some young intern or staff assistant. Instead, Hysom had been around a while, working in Adam Schiff's office for years before becoming chief of staff for Auchincloss. Schiff had performed Tim Hysom's marriage to his husband.

It bothered me that a biological male was threatening me, a 5'2" woman. It bothered me even more that the DOJ was protecting him, refusing to prosecute, and dropping charges for a crime captured on video. Clearly, I wasn't going to get justice under the law. To make matters worse, Jake Auchincloss refused to fire Tim Hysom, even though their office was only a few floors above mine, and he was caught on camera twice. Hysom worked in my building every day and walked in my office halls without any accountability.

I took Hysom's arrest warrant and pictures and made another sign, just as big as the male/female sign, and put it up in the hallway. I made it clear who vandalized my sign and even put "Wanted!" on it!

Naturally, the media put out reports that I was attacking a gay man. Yes, that's right, after he'd repeatedly damaged my property

and was arrested for it, they tried to make *me* the bad guy for harassing *him*. As far as I know, Hysom didn't face any repercussions for his
actions other than some embarrassment from my sign. I already knew
about the media bias, but this showed very clearly that rule of law
doesn't apply when you have powerful friends—namely Auchincloss,
whose father had a very high-level job with the National Institute of
Health alongside Dr. Fauci, and of course Adam Schiff. Hysom's
protectors likely knew a lot of people at the DOJ, and they no doubt
helped protect Hysom from the consequences of his actions.

Sometime later, Stephen Colbert and his film crew got caught in
my building, again by my camera, after they'd been parading around
filming without permission. They were standing in front of my sign
when Capitol Police caught them and kicked them out. And guess
who let them in the building? Tim Hysom and Auchincloss.[46] Were
there any consequences? Silly question!

To me, this wasn't really about a sign. This was about the fact
that I was harassed, my property damaged for speaking the truth,
and that someone with powerful friends could get away with a crime
because he knew the people who pulled the strings. This is the climate that conservatives face when standing against the insanity of
the Left and their trans agenda. That's just the tip of the iceberg
because this was just my own personal introduction to this fight.

Protecting Our Kids

One of the most fundamental biological truths we learn from the
beginning of the Bible is that there are two—and just two—genders.
Male and female. It's the foundation of God's creation that male and
female organisms reproduce together. God created us that way, made
us in His image, and commanded that we go forth and produce little

versions of ourselves; whether we're humans, animals, or even plants, God commanded us to go forth and multiply.

I believe the current attack against gender is wholly evil, aimed at one of the most foundational aspects of God's creation. The Democrat attack on this fundamental aspect of our creation is also evil, and it's a direct attack on God and the Christian faith.

God doesn't need us to defend Him, but in fighting this destructive and unnatural trans agenda, we are fighting against an attack on our faith in God. We're defending the truth of creation in addition to women's rights. But I haven't even gotten to the worst of it. As disgusting as it is to have men in women's private spaces and men winning against women in competition (competitions that have prevented the use of steroids in order to get the same advantage these men have in women's sports), we're also in a fight to protect the most vulnerable of any human—our children.

The most frightening part of all this is the predation of our children, who are being sexualized from a young age and inappropriately introduced to adult concepts. In my mind, young children should not be exposed to the gender-twisting, sexualized depravity these people normalize and even put in books for little kids to read. Even worse, however, is that this twisting of children's minds sometimes results in the mutilation of their bodies, and I will never *ever* be silenced or stop fighting against people who harm children!

Due to the frightening nature of this fight and the life-altering stakes at play, I have written a bill called the Protect Children's Innocence Act—my signature legislation. This could very well be the most important thing I do in my political career, and it's not hyperbole to say that it may be one of the most vital pieces of legislation in decades.

At its core, the bill makes it a class C federal felony for anyone—doctors, nurses, therapists, or anyone else—to be involved in any aspect of a child under eighteen receiving gender therapy. Erroneously called "gender-affirming care," the Left has tried to call radical mastectomies, hysterectomies, castrations, puberty blockers, and hormone treatments a "right" for children—*children!*—who want to transition to another gender. The bill would prohibit any federal funding of any organization or other entity that would perform genital mutilation surgeries. There's nothing "affirming" about castrating a small boy or performing a hysterectomy on a little girl. It is child abuse!

These procedures have life-long repercussions, and young people who transitioned are beginning to come forward to testify about the trauma, pain, and damage they've experienced in the name of gender-affirming care. These precious lives have been damaged, or even ruined, by these procedures. Because the trans movement has such a loud voice for such a tiny sliver of the population (not to mention the full support of the child abusers in the Democrat party), we must take a stand *now*, drawing a line in the sand. Adults may do absurd things to themselves, but they must *not* be allowed to mutilate our children!

The Protect Children's Innocence Act received nearly fifty co-sponsors, and conservative media outlets and personalities got on board to promote it.[47] In addition, we obtained significant support and endorsements from groups like Turning Point, CPAC, and Heritage Foundation.

I also invited a courageous person for the introductory press conference, Chloe Cole—before she became famous for her condemnation of gender transitions for minors. Treated with puberty blockers from the age of thirteen, Chloe had gender dysphoria and wanted to be a man. She later had a double mastectomy in her mid-teens, but that was before she began to realize the tragic mistake she'd made.

Chloe was about eighteen when she bravely spoke at the press conference and told the story of taking puberty blockers and the horrendous surgeries she endured. Living in California, her parents had no right to stop it, and the state offered no safety net. Bear in mind, children's brains don't fully develop until their early twenties, and they can't make life-defining choices alone—they're just kids. No one helped her in her confusion and crisis, and by the time she realized that she was born a woman and needed to *be* a woman, she'd already been mutilated by overzealous health professionals and betrayed by a broken and abusive system.

Chloe began by speaking out on social media and has become more vocal about the dangers these horrible procedures pose to minors. She was incredibly moving in her first full public speaking appearance, telling her story in front of the Capitol as I introduced a bill designed to protect girls and boys like her from the predators who are sexualizing and mutilating our children.

The Protect Children's Innocence Act is so important because Democrats are attacking *children* and destroying their sense of identity and gender. They're trying to normalize the sexualization and grooming of minors—and make us accept it as normal. Not only that, they're also trying to take away parents' rights to protect their kids, especially in states like California and Washington. Those states are branding themselves as "trans child sanctuary states," but what they're really doing is taking away parents' rights and mutilating children! They're destroying people's lives before they've hardly even begun. Some states are taking children *away from their families* and putting them in foster homes. At the same time, they undergo these mutilative surgeries and treatments!

Already a multi-billion-dollar industry, the predation of our children has become big money under the guise of healthcare. It disgusts me that hospitals and large medical organizations that may receive federal support are targeting our most vulnerable group.[48]

You would think that every sane conservative or even moderate in government would get on board with protecting our kids, but I'm shocked and saddened to say this is not the case. Some of the best conservatives in Congress are not rushing to defend our children from true evil.

I'm a big believer in states' rights. Still, when a state's terrible laws disenfranchise parents, separate families, and abuse children with undeniable child abuse procedures, we must pass federal laws to protect our kids. The states' rights issue has become one of the biggest arguments against my bill—ironically from some of the most conservative members of Congress. Members of the Freedom Caucus, who I believed were solid conservative Christians and would be the *first* to protect our children, balked against the bill because it would supersede states' legislation that permits this inexcusable child abuse.

It's up to voters to hold their representatives accountable and demand that we take action to stop the damage being done to our children. It's not okay to hide behind calling it a states' rights issue; we must take action to put a stop to this *now*.

Pedophiles

One of my most controversial statements came out during a 60 Minutes interview. I boldly called Democrats who promote the abuse of children in this matter *pedophiles*. Is that strong language? Definitely! But according to Merriam-Webster's dictionary, the definition of pedophilia is the "sexual perversion in which children are the preferred sexual object," and that is *precisely* what this is. Sexualizing children is absolutely perversion. Of course, every Democrat takes exception to this bold declaration. They sexualize children and take power from parents to protect their kids. It must be stopped.

Pramila Jayapal introduced a resolution she would love to make into federal law, a Trans Bill of Rights, giving children the right to transgender surgeries—paid for by the American people, of course. Sure, they can't smoke or drink, or sometimes even drive yet, but she wants them to be able to decide, as children, to transition to another gender—and for you and me to pay for it! Additionally, she wants transgender people to be assured of having housing, jobs, medical care, and trans education.[49]

Together with the Equality Act, this Trans Bill of Rights is one of the most dangerous pieces of legislation I've seen. These disgusting efforts to promote pedophilia and the abuse and disfigurement of our children are genuine threats, and they're not going away soon. That's why it's so important to protect our kids and do anything we can to prevent these laws!

Sick and perverted people are coming for our kids. There's not only a flag for trans but also for those calling themselves "*minor-attracted*."[50] Yes, you read that right—they're trying to normalize being *sexually attracted* to *children*! Soon, will people be able to justify their pedophilia by claiming it's a lifestyle choice, like being gay or trans? That thought terrifies me for our kids. Think I'm exaggerating? In 2021, the San Francisco Gay Men's Choir sang a song with the lyrics, "We're coming for your children."[51] Look it up—it's frightening. They speak of tolerance, but they're singing of preying on children's sexuality.

Just look at Washington State and recent legislation signed by Governor Jay Inslee, Senate Bill 5599, which destroys parental rights and enables our youth to participate in self-mutilating gender surgery.

The fight for "trans rights" is an agenda promoted by the Left and the Democrat party, and it is not just about tolerance; it's about conversion, sexualization, exploitation, and mutilation. In the face of this threat, the Republican's lack of coordinated, urgent response illustrates everything that's wrong with the Republican party right now. Will we let the issue of states' rights prevent us from stopping this insanity and the threat to innocent children? We need to step up!

The Left speaks of tolerance, but they have no tolerance for our rights or our children's. They do not respect our beliefs or the values of Christianity. They have no respect for marriages, families, or what these gender-bending ideas do to people. They have no respect for our children and are paving the way for pedophiles to groom them, sexualize them, abuse them, and mutilate them. How long until Democrats try to make "minor-attracted" a legitimized lifestyle choice? Well, you won't have to wait very long. In Minnesota, a trans lawmaker introduced a piece of legislation that would include pedophilia as a protected sexual orientation.

This will not stop.

So, the question is, will *we* stop them? Will we make laws that will protect our kids . . . or permit their exploitation? Will we preserve their innocence or expose them to perversion and predation?

Make no mistake; this is an attack on the core foundation of our society. They've already worked to destroy marriage, but now they're attacking our identity. It's an attack on girls and women, children, and even against God and His design of human beings.

The devil attacked Eve in the Garden of Eden, and Adam wasn't there to help or protect her. Isolated, she wasn't strong enough to resist his lies and temptations. I am a strong, independent woman who has proved my capabilities. Still, I definitely know that men brimming with testosterone are bigger and stronger than I am (notice, I didn't say smarter or more valuable). Being stronger wouldn't have helped Adam against the devil, but now people in a position of strength have a responsibility to protect women and girls because this is an attack directed right at us. They want to take our sports, our culture, and our *safety*.

I believe that Satan hates women and our ability to produce life, and it is no mistake that attacks like the Equality Act and the Trans Bill of Rights destroy women and our safety. They want girls to think they must be big and muscular to be strong, like men, and they want boys to think they need to be effeminate to be sensitive and caring. It's just not true. We don't need to be each other's gender; we can each be who God created us to be.

In the wake of COVID, we had protests in which Antifa destroyed the rule of law. Antifa, and other similar groups, are already on board with drag queen story time. They lead counter-protests, fighting conservatives and Christians standing up against this sick insanity. I hate to imagine these anarchists rioting in the streets, trying to terrify and intimidate people who resist the trans agenda.

There are already calls for violent trans protests and attacks. Audrey Hale, the twenty-eight-year-old trans woman who attacked a Nashville Christian school in March of 2023, had a manifesto in her car when she shot and killed three adults as well as three nine-year-old children.[52] The Left wants to blame white supremacist gun owners for mass shootings, so the legacy media tried to cover up Hale's motivations for the shooting. But the evidence points to a troubled young woman who blamed Christians enough to go on a senseless, murderous rampage. Angry trans mobs have also attacked people like Riley Gains, trying to silence their free speech when it's against their agenda.

What adults do together sexually is their business—and should be kept to themselves. Interestingly, many gay people also agree with me that targeting our kids is wrong. Groups like Gays Against Groomers and the Log Cabin Republicans have publicly sided with us against the sexualization of children and the Equality Act.

I am not passive or tolerant when they try to come after kids and mutilate them. That is abject evil; I will fight it with all I have! This is not just Left vs. Right; this is good against evil. Most Democrat voters agree that children should not be sexualized, groomed, or have transgender surgeries as minors. Independent and Republican voters strongly agree, showing that we can come together on this issue and protect our kids.

But the radical Left, which I am convinced is evil, is out for complete control of the Democrat party, and they've made trans issues their top agenda item. Joe Biden, who lied and ran as a moderate, has taken the matter up himself and has promoted sexualizing and disfiguring children under the guise of gender-affirming care.

This is perhaps *the* battle of our generation, and the entire leadership of the Democrat party has sided with the pedophiliac child abusers that want to mutilate children. We must protect them! What they do after turning eighteen is their own business as adults, but until that age, no child needs to be transitioned, sexualized, or abused. No hormones, puberty blockers, hysterectomies, or castrations—no violence against kids should be acceptable.

Yet Republicans continue to be weak, refusing to take a stand because they're arguing about states' rights or are afraid they will offend someone. This is a prime example of why we're losing our country. Republicans are constantly weak regarding the health of our children, refusing to fight against the most insidious enemy we've seen in our lifetime, the Democrat party.

If Republicans do not stop this transgender movement right now, it will grow into one of the most evil things we've ever seen in history. One report said that the number of kids who identify as transgender has doubled in five years. While only 0.6 percent of adults identify as trans, it's supposedly gone from 0.7 percent to 1.4 percent among kids aged thirteen to seventeen.[53] Unfortunately, that's not going to slow down anytime soon, as more kids are exposed to this gender-bending lunacy.

In a decade, we'll see so many young people in their twenties and thirties with *life-long* medical problems from the mutilating transgender surgeries, damaging puberty blockers, and hormone treatments. They'll be people like Chloe Cole, who regretted what she'd done but now receives hate speech for speaking out. They're called "de-transitioners," and few seem to be listening to their warnings right now. Unfortunately, by the time more people are suffering from these procedures, it will be too late to save them the pain and suffering Chloe and others have gone through.

Can we, in good conscience, let our kids go through this when we could prevent their exploitation, sexualization, grooming, and mutilation? These aren't just words—this is what is happening now every day.

I won't be silenced; I will do whatever I can to fight this evil, and I welcome everyone who will join me to oppose this child abuse with the legislation that can close the door on the trans agenda and protect our children's innocence. As the Bud Light fiasco showed us, the American people are going to have to be the louder voice.

8

House Freedom Caucus

THE HOUSE FREEDOM CAUCUS (HFC) is filled with many good people, many of whom I like. I will always be thankful to the House Freedom Caucus for supporting and joining my efforts in roll-calling votes and putting Congress on record for the first time in years. I really enjoyed being a member of the HFC when we fought against the Democrat leadership that ran the House like a communist dictatorship. We were unified to fight the Democrats and their immoral, America-last policies.

But sadly, things changed for the 118th Congress after I, along with Jim Jordan and over half of the Freedom Caucus, supported Kevin McCarthy for speaker.

The effort to go against Kevin McCarthy started last Congress (the 117th Congress) or possibly before. The plans had been made before we won back the majority in 2022, and, at one time, I supported it. As a new freshman in Congress, I was repeatedly told to remember that Kevin McCarthy kicked me off my committees on February 4, 2021. And I believed the HFC leadership, members, and certain Conservative Partnership Institute members who kept reminding me.

More than a year later, in the summer of 2022, I was talking with Devin Nunes, who heard me say Kevin McCarthy kicked me off my committees. He reacted quickly, telling me that was not true, explaining he was in the room watching Kevin McCarthy yell at Steny Hoyer not to kick me off committees. Since then, other Republican members in the room have confirmed that Kevin McCarthy didn't kick me off my committees.

Discovering the truth in the summer of 2022 changed my perspective of McCarthy. I dislike being lied to, and I had been lied to repeatedly., I realized this was an effort by the HFC to make sure I hated Kevin McCarthy and aimed my fire at him and Republican leadership. I came to understand that is how the HFC works. Every meeting and conversation is filled with messaging that Republican leadership is the enemy and you're a sellout or RINO if you dare work with them.

When I found out I had been lied to, I had a realization. I wanted to serve my district and my country and change the Republican party to one that will serve America first and best. As only 1 of 435 members of Congress, I couldn't do that alone. I needed to start networking among the other Republican members of Congress—not just a small, inclusive group, but all of them. I came here to serve my district and my country, and I couldn't do that by serving a small inclusive group within the Republican party. That's not what I came here to do.

In the second half of 2022, while still maintaining my strong conservative values and voting record, I spent months networking among Republicans and talking with Kevin McCarthy. I was able to explain how the base feels, discuss ideas, hold strategy sessions of how to win the majority, and share ideas about why our Republican party needs to be more conservative and more America First. To my surprise, he agreed with me much of the time.

After the general election in November 2022, we had won a razor-thin majority of 222 seats. Bob Good reached out to me, sharing he had formed an HFC group and was organizing an effort to stop Kevin McCarthy from being Speaker of the House. Bob asked me to commit to voting against McCarthy for Speaker in order to attend their meetings. I replied that I could not commit to that and would not participate in any of the meetings. I knew these plans had been laid long ago, and the only basis of the plan was "Never Kevin," which is no plan at all. Just like "Never Trump" is not a plan but continues to be a bad problem in the Republican party.

I chose to support Kevin McCarthy for several reasons. Kevin McCarthy was the only Republican that consistently told the conference that he wanted to be Speaker and was the only Republican that ever made all the necessary steps to become Speaker of the House. This included an agenda and setting fundraising records to win the majority throughout the '22 cycle. To even have a shot at the gavel, you must prove you can win it, and Kevin McCarthy proved it. Whether you agree with every Republican member is not a requirement; it is winning a minimum of 218 Republican seats that gets you a shot at holding the gavel.

As the minority leader of the 117th Congress, he led us to victory. Kevin was also the only one who had earned the majority of support of Republicans from every shade and every ideology. This support garnered respect from Republicans for his hard work and efforts to win a majority and the gavel that gave every Republican power, including HFC members.

It must be recognized that President Trump plays the biggest role in Republican races; his endorsement is the golden seal that tells conservatives which candidates they should vote for. Smaller groups, like the House Freedom Fund, fundraise and support Republican candidates as well. But even the most ardent Never Keviners like Scott Perry, Lauren Boebert, and Bob Good took hundreds of thousands and even millions in their campaigns directly from and through the help of Kevin McCarthy.

Yet the Never Kevin group gave no thought, no care, and no respect to the fact that without Kevin McCarthy's leadership, record-setting fundraising efforts, campaign support, and teamwork with the rest of the leadership and the NRCC, none of us would have the gavel. Nor would we have the committee power, subpoena power, budget and appropriations power, control over the NDAA, ability to write the five-year Farm Bill, and freedom from Nancy Pelosi's reign from hell.

It was only after the November 2022 election, and the Never Kevin group had been officially formed, that Andy Biggs announced that he was running for Speaker of the House with no plan and no agenda. Not to mention, our razor-thin Republican majority was less than two months away from taking power, and Biggs had no ability to fundraise.

As much as I like Andy Biggs and share his conservative values, you would have to be a fool to believe this was a serious effort or plan to become third in line to the president. Holding the gavel includes organizing the entire managerial structure of not only the Capitol but also all the House committees—and this was all less than two months away. Not to mention, Speakership would require Andy Biggs to raise enough money for every Republican member to get re-elected and win more Republican seats going into a presidential year. Being on the bottom tier of fundraisers, Andy had no evidence to show he was capable of raising the money it would require to win an even bigger majority in 2024.

I announced weeks before the Speaker's vote that I supported Kevin McCarthy for Speaker and spent many interviews and social media posts explaining why. I always explain and defend my position once I've made a decision. I felt it was the right thing to do for my district and the country, all in hopes of swaying others to see the playing field as clearly as I could.

Republican voters from across the country had just worked so hard to win us the majority. I was not willing to gamble with Speaker votes and risk losing the gavel to Democrats because a group of my friends practically took a Never Kevin blood oath. The Never Kevin group was cemented together by past grudges dating back to when the Freedom Caucus unseated John Boehner stopped Kevin's first attempt at Speaker, ultimately making Paul Ryan Speaker of the House.

Political terrorist plots by the House Freedom Caucus have had very few victories, but making Paul Ryan Speaker of the House was all Freedom Caucus. And to this day, Paul Ryan's Speakership is the one that most conservatives despise. This was another reason I would have no part in the Never Kevin group; it was only based on hate for Kevin McCarthy, and they had no real plan.

The House Freedom Caucus members and I share many of the same conservative dreams. We align on how Congress should be run and what conservative principles we should strive for in Congress. Most Freedom Caucus members and, actually, most Republicans in Congress (including Kevin McCarthy) agree on important issues such as:

- Balancing the budget
- Reducing our national debt
- Reducing the size of our out-of-control, over-bloated government
- Reducing our dependence on foreign countries like China
- Improving US economic strength
- Building strong, secure borders
- Providing safe, good education for our children
- Protecting the lives of the unborn and children all the way to adulthood
- Becoming energy independent, and maintaining American energy independence

These issues, I believe, should be the basis of our Republican party's platform.

None of this can be achieved by a small, insurgent group of approximately twenty House Republican members aggressively attacking their own conference. The reality is that it takes 218 members of Congress voting yes to pass anything in the House. Insurgent attacks only lead to division, resentment, mistrust, and eventually hate among the conference. No, the only way to achieve this worthy Republican platform is by aggressively winning the White House, the Senate, and as many seats in the House as possible. I had come to this conclusion quickly in my freshman year after being part of the insurgent group.

In late November of 2022, it was easy for me to see that the type of legislation we produced, committee work we took on, investigations we led, and the agenda we set for the American people was the work of the whole conference together. The conference has to be led by a Speaker, who can do the hardest job of all—get Republicans to agree with each other. I saw no need to be part of a Never Kevin plot doomed to failure; I only saw the need to roll up my sleeves and get to work in my conference to achieve my agenda. This meant doubling my efforts to get President Trump back in the White House, win the Senate, and win as many seats as possible in the House in 2024. This didn't make me a RINO; this made me one of the biggest elephants in Washington, a real Republican hell-bent on shaping the Republican party to be the party that saves America—no matter who I have to fight to get there.

While over half of the Freedom Caucus supported Kevin McCarthy for Speaker, the leadership members of the HFC were angry at me, and oddly, just me. They talked amongst themselves about kicking me out and even met with me about it.

I was shocked and couldn't understand why I was their target. In the HFC, either you hate Kevin McCarthy and fight leadership at all times, or you're not being a good obedient HFC member. Hating leadership is the Kool-Aid they offer, and it's passed around like communion at every HFC meeting. But for some reason, the core group, which is mainly the HFC board members, was just mad at me. Not Jim Jordan, who was nominated multiple times during the speaker's race by HFC members. Had he been Speaker of the House, Jim Jordan could not have served on the House Judiciary Committee and instead would have had to focus ninety percent of his efforts on fundraising around the country, a role he expressly did not want. There was no ire directed towards Mark Green, Warren Davidson, or any more than half of House Freedom Caucus members who supported and voted for Kevin McCarthy. Nope, they were mainly just vehemently mad at *me*.

But why just me? After all, this is a group that does hold grudges even though the HFC is founded on Christian principles, and forgiveness is a pillar of being a Christian. Even though I have forgiven, I don't think many of them have.

Perhaps for the first time, they found themselves at the losing end of a battle because I was on the other side. Or maybe they felt betrayed by my audacity to develop an opinion of my own and act on it outside the groupthink of the HFC. One way of saying it could be that I developed a tolerance to the Kool-Aid, and it didn't affect me anymore. I have always been an independent thinker who makes decisions based on the reality that lies before me, the potential of the wins that lie ahead, and the tools I have available.

The HFC had cheered me on until the Speaker race, which went a historic fifteen rounds in the first week of our majority in January 2023. Before the race, the House Freedom Fund used my name and likeness to raise tens of millions of dollars to elect conservative members of Congress—a role I gladly allowed and freely gave without asking for anything in return.

I played the top role next to Jim Jordan in fundraising for HFC candidates (including the new freshman who are now HFC members) and the chairman and board members (who I had also voted for); they were some of the top beneficiaries of money that was raised in my name, while I selflessly received almost nothing. I must admit, it doesn't feel good to be treated like an outsider after happily supporting everyone else in fundraising to get elected and re-elected.

After the speaker's race, HFC meetings were uncomfortable. I didn't like the side glances that came my way or being treated like an outsider. And when I asked for support from the HFC on bills and ideas, they were quickly tossed to the side.

I could never understand why I could not get the House Freedom Caucus to support my bill, the Protect Children's Innocence Act. My bill would make it a felony to perform genital mutilation procedures on anyone under 18, giving minors puberty blockers and hormone treatments, and would protect parent's rights to stop the evil and barbaric practice of amputating teenage girls' breasts and castrating adolescent boys. I repeatedly asked for HFC to take an official position in support of my bill, and they repeatedly refused.

The only explanations I ever received were from Scott Perry and Chip Roy, who both argued that these horrific surgeries and permanently damaging medical treatments were a "states' rights" issue, not a federal one. I argued each time that this had to be a federal issue; parents in states like California were having their children taken away by the state when they tried to intervene and stop the evil transmedical community from barbarically destroying their children.

But this wasn't the only time I disagreed with Scott Perry, the Chair of the HFC, and Chip Roy, an HFC board member. I was a new freshman in Congress and a new member of the Freedom Caucus when I first fought with Chip Roy. I argued with him, urging him to object to Joe Biden's electoral college votes like over 130 other Republicans did, including Kevin McCarthy. Instead, Chip Roy voted to validate Joe Biden's presidency and now supports Ron DeSantis for president. He clearly doesn't like my favorite president. While I believe everyone can choose who they want for president, I can't understand his lack of support for my bill to stop the genital mutilation of children. It is not a states' rights issue, it's a child abuse issue, and while we have plenty of federal laws on child abuse, we need this one, too.

Scott Perry also argued with me, claiming it is a states' rights issue. Again, it is not. However, Scott Perry also voted for gay marriage in late 2022, just before the general election. (I voted against it, along with many Republicans, including Kevin McCarthy.) It was an outrage among many House Freedom Caucus donors that the chairman of the Freedom Caucus voted for gay marriage. Instead of standing on principle and voting against it, he apparently was more concerned about his re-election chances and voted for it. Oddly, there was no motion to kick *him* out of the Freedom Caucus or remove him from the chair. When the bill was brought back to the floor from the Senate, he voted against gay marriage, but that was after he had won his re-election.

Yet the biggest tell-tale sign that the board of the HFC didn't care about rules, quorums, order, or conservative and constitutional principles is this: They called for an impromptu meeting at 8 a.m. on June 23, 2023—a fly out day—and held a vote to kick me out of the Freedom Caucus because I called Lauren Boebert a bitch to her face in a private conversation on the House floor. They did this without a quorum being present and after some members had left after speaking against their proposed vote. I wasn't even there to defend myself or give my side of the story. Hours later, while in the House chamber conducting our last votes of the week, I found out about their vote on Twitter. Not one single HFC member came up to me to tell me.

When I saw the news, I walked over to another HFC member and asked if the vote had happened, and he confirmed it did. He shared that Scott Perry told everyone in attendance that he had tried to reach me, but I never returned any of his calls or texts. The truth was I did not have one single call or text from Scott Perry on either of my phones, both of which I had on me at that very moment. The entire time we were in the House chamber, Scott Perry never walked over to inform me about what happened. Instead, he sent another HFC member over to me after votes to ask if I would talk with Scott Perry in a private room off the chamber floor.

I was furious at that point and said no. I had a scheduled meeting with the Speaker of the House, Kevin McCarthy, and his staff to talk about my bill, the Protect Children's Innocence Act. Ironic that it was the same bill that the HFC refused to support and Scott Perry and Chip Roy claimed was a states' rights issue. There was absolutely no way I would miss an important meeting with the Speaker of the House about the one bill I care about most in order to have an unplanned talk about ridiculous, high school-level drama.

It was absurd and childish for them to try to drag me to a private room to inform me that I had been voted out after they had already done it. Especially on a hectic fly-out day. We're all scrambling to finish up before rushing to the airport to catch flights to our home districts.

This all began when I drafted my articles of impeachment on Joe Biden for causing a national security and humanitarian crisis at the border through his border policies. I asked Lauren Boebert and all the House Freedom Caucus to cosponsor my articles of impeachment. Instead of cosponsoring mine, she wrote her own and introduced them a few weeks later. She told leadership that she had to do it to help her end-of-quarter fundraising, and then she abruptly brought her resolution to the floor without ever addressing the conference or asking for support. Remember, it takes 218 Republicans voting together to pass anything. Then she tried to force it to a vote through a privileged resolution. I told the media how she had copied my articles of impeachment.

Lauren walked up to me on the House floor, demanding I clarify the comments I had made to the press, at which point I called her a "little bitch" to her face. After I told her what I thought of her, I told Lauren to shut up and that the only person recognized to speak was Anna Paulina, which ended our conversation.

That conversation took place between the two of us, and no one would have ever known what we said to each other if Lauren had not leaked it to the media. After walking away, Lauren texted a reporter at a leftist gossip blog that attacks Republicans. As Anna Paulina Luna (also a member of the House Freedom Caucus) started speaking, I sat back down in my seat next to another Republican member of Congress. Minutes later, he received a text from a reporter asking if he had heard me call Lauren Boebert a "bitch." He asked me if it was okay to tell him, and I said yes, because Lauren was already leaking the story. I have no respect for leakers, only those who openly tell the truth 100% of the time. When I walked off the House floor, I was swarmed by the press, who, to my surprise, knew every detail of our "private" conversation. When they asked me if it was true, I answered that it was "impressively correct." And it was only impressively correct because Lauren herself had delivered all the details by text to a liberal blog before we had even walked off the House floor.

The press love drama and gossip, and me calling Lauren Boebert a bitch became the top headline in the news that day and remained a big topic of conversation the rest of the week, even bigger than her impeachment stunt. It also became the petty little reason that the HFC decided to hold a last-minute vote at the end of that week to kick me out without ever hearing my side of the story. They only believed that Lauren was the victim, a "victim" who leaked the story to the press herself.

This situation was problematic for the HFC because Lauren Boebert is their communications chair and sits on the board but leaked to the press. But it was a bigger problem for the HFC when you look at it as a business decision. They kicked me out and kept her, and that was not a good financial decision.

I was the second-highest fundraiser for the HFC and never kept nor asked for any of the money for myself. I have also paid all my dues to the NRCC and, as I write, have donated another $100,000 to support Republicans winning in 2024. I also raised my own money to campaign with and easily won my 2022 election with 66% of the vote. I am not a drain or a problem member to get reelected, and fortunately, I represent a wonderful red district.

However, Lauren Boebert almost lost her seat in 2022 and barely won by just over 500 votes in a red district with a rating of R+7. She is constantly a big recipient of money from HFC donors, and polling shows she does not have good support from Republican voters in her district. She also asks for support from the NRCC and Kevin McCarthy's fundraising efforts while she constantly fights Kevin McCarthy and does things to upset the entire conference. Going into 2024, she will be a significant financial lift for HFC donors to support and get reelected unless she turns things around with her district. But her actions have created other problems; she has made many enemies, and they won't want to help her out of the challenging situation she has put herself in.

It's not fair to all the good, hard-working House Freedom Fund donors who contribute a lot of money to support conservatives getting elected in Congress. It is especially unfair because Lauren Boebert and I have almost an identical voting record, and at the end of the day, that is the only thing that should matter. But it didn't matter to the HFC board members and the core group of HFC that kicked me out. They should have cared about conservative votes and legislation, not silly arguments that were supposed to be private and could have been worked out if Lauren had not leaked it to the press.

The Lauren Boebert argument was just an excuse to do what they wanted to do all along—kick me (and only me) out because I supported Kevin McCarthy for Speaker.

With that said, if Kevin McCarthy ever turns back on the promises he made to me as well as the American people, I'll be the first to call it out and hold him accountable.

The problem now is that the HFC acts like an angry cult and wants to kick out its members if they don't hate who they are told to hate and do everything the cult tells them to do. The leadership board and some HFC members are so blinded by their self-righteous mission that they have forgotten that other HFC members and I share the same conservative goals and want to achieve the same great things for our country. Blinded by their self-righteousness, they refuse to recognize that we are all equal individuals with our own ideas on how to achieve conservative goals in Congress. This has also led to judging others and division. And division is wrong, just like it's wrong for the Church to be divided.

But the HFC *wants* to be divided. The same core group that decided to kick me out has always believed that the HFC functions best when it's a small group of insurgents. They don't want to be a big group. They don't want to add more conservative members to the HFC. They just want to be a tiny group with one groupthink mentality. This is the opposite of how our Founding Fathers formed Congress to work and is why the HFC will ultimately continue to fail.

United we stand, and divided we fall. We can never defeat the Democrats—the real enemy—if we are divided.

It has taken decades for our country to fall into the despair we find ourselves in now. Operating in a burn-it-all-down mentality and turning everyone against each other won't save the country. It will take many years of diligent, dedicated work to lift ourselves back up to be the country we want to hand to our children.

That requires Republicans to hold the majority in the House, win the Senate, and win the White House with President Trump and more like him in the years to come. That means Republicans must work out our problems and collaborate to convince the American people to trust our party to solve our country's problems.

We will never be able to solve our country's problems if we constantly fight and treat each other as the enemy instead of fighting the Democrats, who are the enemies of the American people.

I don't want to burn it all down. I love America and its people. I want to solve our country's problems. I want to save our children's future. I'll fight as hard as I can and diligently work, putting one foot in front of the other, for as long as it takes to save America.

Yet, I cannot change the system alone. For that, I need help, both at home and in Washington. I'm blessed to be on the COVID Select Subcommittee, where we are trying to make changes that will prevent the abuses and government overreach of the pandemic. Still, we cannot do it alone—every voter must stand up and be counted!

9

COVID Lies and Lessons

I UNDERSTAND THE IMMENSE HEARTBREAK and devastation of the COVID pandemic on multiple levels. No one escaped the pandemic without a few scars. Most people lost loved ones and friends or know someone who did. Many who died were older adults with underlying conditions or people with risk factors like obesity, but a few were younger healthy people.

Sitting on the COVID Select Subcommittee in Congress has given me a front-row seat to the details of the debacle that killed many, terrified our citizens, and ravaged our economy. As I begin to learn what we knew and when we knew it, I'm convinced that much of this devastation *didn't need to happen*. What I've found confirmed something I had been kicking and screaming about since day one.

Like many, my parents were frightened by the media regarding COVID and stayed home. They would get the mail with masks and gloves on, take it into the garage, spray it down with Lysol, and then leave it there for three days before opening it. My dad had comorbidities—high blood pressure and heart disease—and they

131

were convinced that if he got the virus, he'd end up on a ventilator and die.

All through 2020, they went nowhere, getting groceries delivered to the car and barely leaving the house—including to go to the doctor. One of the saddest parts was that my dad didn't go to his routine doctor visits for his high blood pressure and cholesterol. He was afraid he'd catch the virus in the waiting room. Many doctors' offices nationwide were shut down, and some hospitals weren't allowing certain procedures. Unfortunately, my father had a spot on his chest that he delayed getting checked because he was so afraid of going to the doctor.

When he finally did go to the doctor, the doctor he saw said it looked fine. By late summer, he had strange symptoms—his energy levels were down, and he had headaches. The headaches got so bad that he would vomit. He even went to the ER several times, but they told him he had vertigo, and he just got sicker.

Towards the end of 2020, he was finally diagnosed with a Stage 4 melanoma that had metastasized to his brain, resulting in multiple brain tumors. My dad actually received the same diagnosis as Jimmy Carter, and as of this writing, Carter is still living. We hoped at the time that Dad would survive melanoma just like Carter had, and they put my father on the same immunotherapy treatment.

I won my election in November 2020, and my father had his first brain surgery to remove the tumors a month later, in December 2020. We were prevented from going into the hospital with him because of COVID restrictions and hospital policies. We couldn't be there to comfort him, encourage him, or hold his hand. We couldn't cry with him or hug him.

During surgery, they would be cutting open his entire skull to reach the tumors, and he was scared to death. The doctors told him that his brain may not work how it used to after surgery. Even if he survived the treatments, he knew his life would never be the same. He fought for his life—*alone*. My mom, his wife of nearly fifty years, couldn't sit with him; neither could my brother or I. My dad faced brain surgery alone, with strangers covered by masks and surgical gear, not a loved one in sight.

Many people across our country shared similar experiences due to the rules imposed during the COVID pandemic. It was devastating, cruel, and should not have happened.

My dad made it through that first surgery. The brain is so delicate, and he was definitely a little different when he came out. He couldn't read anymore, but he could still do a lot.

A few weeks later, I was sworn into Congress, but on January 12, I had to fly back to Washington. We were supposed to be with our district on recess, but Nancy Pelosi called for a vote on the second attempt to impeach President Donald Trump because of the insanity on January 6. This cruel, vindictive, and hateful woman pounced on this opportunity to punish and persecute President Trump.

Flying into Washington to vote *NO* on the impeachment came at a high personal cost. I missed my father's second brain surgery to remove more tumors, which was scheduled the same day that Nancy Pelosi forced us all to return to Washington to vote on her Trump derangement, hate-fueled impeachment number two. It was one of the worst days of my entire life; not only did I miss the surgery, but I had to leave my mom all alone because she couldn't go inside the hospital.

To my lasting grief, my Dad was never the same afterward, and by the time I got back, he was changed. I've always been a daddy's girl. He was the one I came to for advice, and I talked with my dad more than anyone else, including my then-husband. He'd always been there for me to lean on.

My father hung on, always a fighter. He continued taking medications and the immunotherapy treatments Jimmy Carter took. He and my mom even happily took the COVID vaccines, believing they should and would be able to go out in public more if Dad got better.

But he didn't get better; he got worse. The cancer spread throughout his body quickly.

I helped my mother make the decision that it was time for home hospice care. I think that was the best decision. We took Dad home from the hospital and lovingly cared for him during the last days of his life. And when Mom was giving out, I took care of both of them. It was one of the hardest things I've ever done—and one of the best things I've ever done.

On April 11, 2021, our whole family gathered around my dad in my parent's bedroom, and we all told stories about him. My mom shared the best stories. We all laughed, cried, and remembered so many treasured times. We could hold my father's hand and feel him hold our hands back, even though he looked like he was resting peacefully. I believe to this day, he listened to all our stories and loved every minute. I also believe it helped him let go; he knew he was loved, and he heard us all tell our memories of what an amazing husband, father, and man he had been to us.

Just after midnight, my mother was in the bathroom getting ready for bed, my brother and sister-in-law were asleep, and my children had all gone home for the night. I lay on the bed next to my father and watched his spirit leave his body. It was so fast. He just got up and went. He was finally ready and went so quickly because he knew where he was going. It was the most amazing thing I've ever seen—something I can hardly describe, but something I can see in my mind like it just happened.

In the early morning hours on April 12, 2021, my father went home to Heaven and was pronounced dead. The men that came to prepare his body were kind and gentle. They put him in a casket and draped it with an American flag because he had served in the Navy and was a Vietnam combat veteran. They carried his body out of the house in the flag-draped casket.

The following week, as my mother grieved, I helped her plan every detail of his funeral and burial. And, truth be told, I just took over. She was completely exhausted and broken from months and months of fighting cancer with Dad. It was devastating and horrible.

My father's entire cancer battle, which finally ended in his death, took place in just over five months, from the end of 2020 into the spring of 2021. It all coincided with my first few months in Congress and the worst media attacks any member of Congress has ever been through. I faced January 6, President Trump's impeachment, being kicked off committees, and the legacy media's unbelievably cruel 24/7 lying, defamatory attacks on me. Almost every single day, my name was on the top headlines. But every single moment, all I could think about was my father dying of cancer.

Those were some of the darkest days of my life, and there are no words to describe the pain I endured. But I can say without a shadow of a doubt that I only made it through because Jesus carried me and God protected me. Not a single arrow penetrated me, nor was a single hair on my head damaged. God gave me incredible strength, and I walked in His great and mighty shadow each moment.

Everything about that time still makes me angry. I'm still angry over the impeachment and even more angry that I had to leave my family during a difficult time. It was a ridiculous lie that Nancy

Pelosi forced us all to participate in. I'm also still angry at the communist policies implemented during the pandemic, taking away people's freedoms in the name of the "common good." It didn't have to be this way—for me, my father, or many other Americans.

Everybody lost during the COVID shutdown—everybody. The shutdowns were completely wrong, and the pandemic was mishandled. They knew the facts about the virus early and which groups it affected most. Dr. Fauci and others knew that masks didn't work, and he even told a friend in a personal email on February 5, 2020, that was later released from a FOIA request:

> "Masks are really for infected people to prevent them from spreading infection to people who are not infected, rather than protecting uninfected people from acquiring infection. The typical mask you buy in the drugstore is ineffective in keeping out a virus small enough to pass through the material. It might, however, provide some slight benefit to keep out gross droplets if someone coughs or sneezes on you. I do not recommend you wear a mask, particularly since you are going to a very low-risk location. Your instincts are correct; your money is best spent on medical countermeasures such as diagnostics and vaccines."[54]

Later, Fauci began urging mask mandates even though he admittedly knew that masking didn't stop the spread of COVID. We knew natural immunity from those who survived the disease was better than vaccine protection. Still, they kept mandating and forcing vaccines and additional boosters—shots that weren't working. How many "vaxxed and boosted" people do you know who got COVID? I know a lot!

Month after month, Americans would see famous politicians like Joe Biden, Kamala Harris, and even former President Barack Hussein Obama publicly get their vaccines and boosters on television to convince the public to get vaccinated . . . then not long afterward, those same famous pro-vaccine, vaccinated, and multi-boosted people would be in the news because they had caught COVID *again*! It was ridiculous, and we all would just shake our heads.

I got the virus in March 2020, and I was sick for about three days. Then I got better . . . and that was it. I was middle-aged and had none of the conditions that put me in the risk group for severe illness, hospitalization, or death. Thankfully, I have always kept a healthy diet and am very dedicated to exercise. Once I had it, I did not catch it again.

In 2021, my then-husband got COVID and became quite ill. His breathing sounded bad, and his blood oxygen level began to drop to nearly 90 percent. I became very worried he would have to go to the hospital. I called the doctor and got him an appointment where they prescribed ivermectin and a full protocol of vitamins. They also sent him in to receive monoclonal antibodies. This combination was a treatment that many doctors were sharing on social media, claiming success at treating COVID and saving countless lives. It worked in less than forty-eight hours. It was a miracle!

My son got COVID one month after he had mononucleosis. I'm sure his immune system was still suppressed and recovering from mono. He was in football season, and it swept through the team. Most of them hardly had symptoms, or their case didn't last long because they were all young, healthy athletes. Again, I called the doctor for my son, and they prescribed him the same ivermectin and vitamin protocol, and in a matter of days, he bounced back.

As a matter of fact, everyone I know who got COVID either had such a mild case, as I did, they just got over it on their own, or they took hydroxychloroquine (HCQ) or ivermectin along with a specific vitamin protocol that included zinc, magnesium, and vitamin D. Everyone I knew recovered well—even a few people who were very advanced in age and had severe comorbidities, including my then-husband's grandmother, who had COVID at ninety-seven years old. She recovered in a week!

I followed Dr. Fauci's advice he gave privately in his personal email, not his public hypocritical advice.[55] I didn't wear a mask. None of my kids wore masks. Most people I knew didn't wear a mask unless it was forced in public or to fly on an airplane. We knew masks didn't work, were filthy, forced you to breathe in your carbon dioxide, and decreased the amount of oxygen in your bloodstream.[56] Many of us felt wearing a mask was like wearing a muzzle.

A few people I know who had the virus got ill again, but they were very mild cases, and they handled it the same way our society used to handle colds and cases of flu: stay home, rest, get well, recover, and go back about your life. In blue states, where they strongly believed in the vaccine, they got boosted repeatedly. They huddled in their homes, afraid to go out and live . . . yet still got sick. They had very different experiences than those with natural immunity and those of us who believed natural immunity was best and that we should handle the COVID pandemic using herd immunity without lockdowns and forced vaccinations.

We may never know the total number of people affected by how we handled the pandemic—not just those who died from the virus, but the quiet cases of collateral damage, like my father's. There were missed appointments, treatments, and healthcare—all to respond to a disease, not like Americans but communists.

A New Way to Campaign

I was campaigning for Congress in 2020 when we acutely became aware of COVID in America. I'd been busy doing events, knocking on doors, and speaking at local political groups such as Second Amendment and women's groups all over my district. Then, suddenly President Trump was in the news, locking down travel to China (and getting called xenophobic for it) and implementing other travel bans. Democrats quickly criticized him, because they resisted anything he did, but I suddenly found my campaigning paused as we implemented fifteen days to slow the spread and "flatten the curve."

Like almost every American, I had been reading up on this novel coronavirus that was getting so much coverage. We didn't know much, and a lot of conflicting information was out there, but even then, we knew that the elderly and those with underlying health conditions were getting hit the hardest. This wasn't news, exactly, because these groups are always hit the hardest, including by ordinary things like the flu.

At the time, I was forty-six and in good health, so I judged my risk was low. I exercised daily and ate right, so I wasn't too worried about it. In our construction company, we let our employees decide. Some were more worried than others.

Construction was deemed essential, so technically, we stayed open—but not really. While we were considered open, none of our job sites could move forward because the inspectors were government employees, and they were at home! All the government offices were shut down. Between missing workers and being unable to get our inspections done, no work was completed. So, even though we were deemed "essential," we were shut down.

Two of my kids came home from college, and my son's high school closed; they all lost their part-time jobs. I had to limit campaign activities, and for a while, we thought there was nothing we could do about it.

I decided to find ways to reach voters with my message. I took to Facebook Live and started recording videos constantly to connect with people in my district. I even ended up door knocking—from about ten feet away from their front doors! I'd host mini rallies in grocery store parking lots from the back of a truck, my voice amplified by large speakers people could hear from inside their cars. This gave me a significant advantage over my opponents, who had stopped campaigning entirely.

We're not easily intimidated in Georgia, and we were the first state to reopen, leading the way for other red states, like Florida, to get back to business. We weren't as shut down as many blue states and got back to work faster, so the impact wasn't as bad in Georgia.

The psychological impact of COVID isn't something we should dismiss. We all endured the shortages of toilet paper and other essentials. Still, in all the locked-down blue states and cities, people were in solitary confinement longer and seemed to experience more lasting impacts from the virus. In the more rational states, those who needed to isolate could do so, such as for health reasons. But many people in Georgia got out again, going to work and socializing responsibly. We weren't locked in our houses for a year or more by ourselves.

Consider for a moment that isolation is used as a form of punishment. We put our most violent prisoners in solitary confinement when their behavior is out of control. Here, Democrat mayors and governors all over the country were doing the same thing to Americans, supposedly for their well-being, by isolating them.

My daughter, who was playing D1 SEC softball on scholarship, had to come home. These college kids are some of the healthiest people in the country, and there was no reason for them to be isolated. The country damaged our young people when their social lives completely ended; they had to come home from school, their sports and activities stopped, and they lost their jobs. We're only now getting the numbers for how significantly the COVID shutdown affected students who were told to teach themselves online during the pandemic. Our kids will be dealing with the loss of in-person education for years, and we may never fully understand its impact on them.

The isolation is a crucial aspect to me. Our seniors couldn't see their kids, and grandparents and great-grandparents died alone or with only staff around them and no loved ones to hold their hands. Meanwhile, we dealt with the fact that our family members were dying without us.

This loss of freedom and government overreach showed the face of communism in America, and I think people should go to jail. It seemed like a terrible double standard favored the political elite while taking away the rights of the rest of us. They took away our freedom to decide for ourselves if it was worth the risk. If a loved one was dying in a hospital or nursing home, I believe that was more important than the risk of spreading COVID.

The entire pandemic response was a gigantic social experiment that failed massively! We could see a drastic difference between the red and blue states, particularly in the rural areas. I saw it regularly as I flew from Rome, Georgia, where I lived, to Washington, DC. In Georgia, schools were open, stores were doing brisk business, and people were free to choose their level of interaction.

In what I started calling the District of Communism, ineffectual and scientifically disproven mask mandates were the norm, schools were closed, store shelves were bare, and it was hard to find something to eat. You couldn't go to a restaurant, few places were open, and many of my meals came from a vending machine! As a member of Congress, I couldn't just hop in my car and pick something up.

And then the vaccine came out. Soon, the mandates started on that, too, and in the District of Communism, you had to show your vaccine card to go into a restaurant, store, and many other places. If you weren't vaccinated with this experimental, rushed vaccine, they prevented you from doing business or buying goods or services. I, and many others, didn't want to be a science experiment, which was my *choice*. I was free to decide, as we all should've been, but in many parts of the country, people were punished if they chose not to let them test the vaccine on them.

They transformed the capital of the District of Communism with National Guard troops, turning it into a giant military base.[57] Just before Joe Biden's inauguration, they locked Washington down, and it looked like a military takeover. Where was this response during the violent Antifa and BLM riots across America?

I'll be honest; it was like living in a prison! I'd never lived like that, with the strict security rules, literal checkpoints, and vaccine and mask mandates. Getting food was especially difficult because I refused to get vaccinated and, because I'm not a liar, would not use a fake vaccine card. Many people I knew paid off doctors to get a vaccine card, so I know that the vaccine numbers they brag about aren't accurate, even in the vaccine stronghold of DC.

If it weren't for the Conservative Partnership Institute (CPI), where many conservatives meet, I'm not sure I would've made it. Just a few blocks from the Capitol, it was an oasis of like-minded people where we could take off our ridiculous, ineffective masks—and, most importantly for me, *eat*! They had a menu set up, and they provided meals for all of us lowly unvaccinated second-class citizens. I could meet with people, work, and fundraise at CPI, out from under the District of Communism's overreaching mandates. It was my home away from home! I would've slept there if I could because this was a little bastion of freedom amid all government overreaching. I never thought I'd be so glad to see a smiling face instead of a mask as I was when I walked into CPI.

Communism showed it was alive and well in America as the government and big tech restricted free speech on the internet. Twitter banned me on January 2, 2022, because I had the gall to constantly speak out about masks, vaccines, and the mandates requiring them.[58] And, let me point out, each of these five things has been proven correct yet was judged as misinformation at the time.

"The controversial #COVID19 vaccines should not be forced on our military for a virus that is not dangerous for non-obese people and those under 65," I tweeted. "With 6,000 vax-related deaths and many concerning side effects reported, the vax should be a choice not mandated for everyone."[59]

"Thousands of people are reporting very serious, life-changing vaccine side effects from taking COVID vaccines," I tweeted out another time. "5,946 deaths are reported on the CDC website. Social media is censoring their stories & the media is silent."[60]

A few days later, I posted, "This is why no entity should force NON-FDA approved vaccines or masks. Instead of help[ing] people protect their health by defeating obesity, which will protect them from COVID complications & death, and many other problems. We should invest in health, not human experimentation."[61]

Finally, I tweeted out, "The FDA should not approve the COVID vaccines. There are too many reports of infection & spread of #COVID19 among vaccinated people. These vaccines are failing

& do not reduce the spread of the virus & neither do masks. Vaccine mandates & passports violate individual freedoms."[62]

These were the tweets that got me banned for a year from my personal campaign Twitter account—the one where I can raise money, put out ads, my personal opinions, and fight back when I get attacked. I still had a Congressional Twitter account. However, that account belongs to the seat of Congress, not me; it just has my name on it currently. By FEC rules, I wasn't allowed to campaign or raise money on that account. So, for sharing the truth, I was banned *during my reelection year!*

With my free speech censored, I had a challenging time raising money for my reelection, and my opponent raised millions more than I did. I was attacked day in and day out. I couldn't defend myself against the lies they spread (no censorship on those, naturally!) as the unholy union of government and big tech conspired to censor conservatives and control the narrative.

It didn't work. I won reelection anyway. I didn't get my Twitter account back until after my election when Elon Musk bought Twitter and began repealing some of the Left's conspiracies to silence dissenting voices. Still, it's a sad commentary on America when we resemble a communist country like China, with the state dictating censorship terms that the tech companies readily agree with.

Never Again

I serve on the COVID Select Committee in Congress, and it feels like we spent a great deal of time rehashing things I thought we already knew. For instance, we knew the origins of the virus early on. Still, because of the lying and posturing in our government, it required the former director of the CDC, Robert Redfield, to testify boldly that it came from a Wuhan lab. The CIA corroborated this, as did many other intelligence agencies, saying they could confirm the origin was a lab in China—just like conservatives were condemned for speaking *from the beginning*. We also know that statements denying we had funded gain of function on coronaviruses were lies, and we have testimony and documentation of the grants dating back at least to 2017 but likely earlier.

We now face difficult choices on the committee; we're tasked with helping ensure the same mistakes don't happen again in any future pandemic. Not only are we wrestling with how the virus began affecting our country, but we must also look at how we addressed it.

The same Democrats who say, "My body, my choice" regarding abortion are all about forcing the vaccines, boosters, and masks on the American people. They championed the government overreach that prevented people from working and going to school, thus wrecking the economy and stunting the development of our students.

Now, we're seeing the effects on the supply chain and inflation. The Democrats took actions to make Americans dependent on government so they'd stay home, and it has fueled record inflation. It has destroyed our economy, people's savings, retirements, and made it increasingly difficult for hard-working Americans to simply put food on the table. The communist policies Democrats pursued under the guise of coping with the pandemic have created a significant economic shift and sent us into recession. However, the Biden administration is trying to redefine the word.

Economically, small businesses may have suffered the most, with thousands shutting down and never reopening. And, God forbid, you were a small investor in real estate and had a few rental properties—the eviction moratorium made it very difficult for anyone depending on that income. I'm afraid we have yet to see the full

impact on our country from these economic policies, as big corporations are only becoming more powerful, and inflation continues to
kill off small businesses. We now see bank closures like we haven't
seen in many years, with bigger banks buying up smaller ones, which
is dangerous for our country's financial security.

When we speak of the future impact, we cannot underestimate
the effect of pandemic-era policies on our kids. Isolated and asked
to self-educate, many are two years behind in their education. Their
test scores dropped, many can't read, and they're going to have a
hard time graduating from high school, let alone getting into college. Depression, anxiety, and suicide rates have soared—all because
liberals thought we had to keep our healthiest citizens home or stuck
behind masks.

It is incredibly frustrating to me that the decisions made for
our kids came from people like Randi Weingarten, who is nothing
more than a political activist for the Left. We let this woman abuse
her power as president of the teacher's union. She was not a doctor,
hadn't taught in years, and isn't even a mother—yet we let her advise
the CDC on when to reopen schools. Her unscientific advice was to
keep schools closed and our kids isolated at home.

The vaccines themselves are a whole other matter. We're only
just now beginning to uncover the numbers of people affected or
even perhaps killed by these vaccines, and big companies like Pfizer,
Moderna, and Johnson & Johnson are not yet being held accountable for the impact these experimental drugs had on people. Yet these
big pharmaceutical companies have deep pockets and make massive
donations through lobbyists.

Many of my fellow members of Congress seem okay to just let
this all go, but I am not! I'm not okay with giving them a pass;
these vaccines need to be investigated, and we need to ask the hard

questions necessary to expose the dangers and problems with them. It's clear from the statistics that part of the population has suffered side effects from these vaccines, yet we're still being pressured to take these same vaccines. How can we mandate our population take these injections when there are consequences, such as myocarditis, blood clots, and other problems that can last a lifetime—or even take lives? These side effects must be studied, and we must ensure that a product is incredibly safe before we force it on people.

The Left can call my demands for studies and accountability "conspiracy theories," but there's too much anecdotal evidence to ignore. We must ask hard questions in our hearings and not let special interests or Big Pharma campaign donations influence our judgment.

The entire pandemic and our response have been a disaster. Obviously, the biggest heartbreak is in the loss of life, and the silent victims, like my father, are even more tragic because it didn't have to happen. These weren't people who got sick and died on a ventilator; they stayed home because they were scared and because the Democrats and their mouthpieces in the media spread fear and lies. Honestly, not one life should have been lost, and it is my belief that COVID is a manmade bioweapon that murdered millions. I hope one day our government will admit that. Everyone suffered as a result.[63] [64] [65] Our economy and kids suffered, too, but we have yet to talk about the unbelievable fraud and waste.

Incredible amounts of money went to foreign countries. Fraud puts countless dollars into people's pockets—so much we don't even know the amount. And Democrats padded the stimulus bills with money for idiocy like Drag Queen Storytime, using federal funds for drug paraphernalia against Congressional precedent, bailout money to failing blue states drowning in debt, and much more pork, graft, and waste.[66]

And those who stood up against this pandemic-induced stupidity? They were derided as conspiracy theorists and, worse, blackballed and shunned. Show contrary evidence on masks that they're harmful to kids? Question vaccine safety? Object to bailout spending? Anyone who dared was attacked.

Nancy Pelosi fined me $2,500[67] every time I stepped on the House floor without a mask, totaling well over $100,000. I matched my words with my actions and stood up for the people of my district, especially children, who overwhelmingly didn't want to be forced to wear masks. I felt I needed to fight the tyrannical mask mandates with actions so that parents and schoolchildren could fight the school boards forcing their children to be wrongfully masked. I believe masking children, especially young children, is a form of child abuse and extremely damaging to their development on many levels.

We knew it then. Not only did masks not stop the spread of COVID, but studies now verify how dangerous it is to breathe carbon dioxide for hours a day. Yet, they wouldn't listen, shot me down, fined me, and made me a pariah for going against the narrative. As I write this, Thomas Massie, Ralph Norman, and I are litigating a lawsuit against Nancy Pelosi for unconstitutionally fining us for not wearing masks on the House floor.

During COVID insanity, I was even bullied for not wearing a mask by many Democrats. One Democrat took it to a whole new level by bullying me and then pretending to be the victim afterward. On the same day I flew to Washington to vote NO on President Trump's impeachment, leaving my mom while my dad had his second brain surgery, I was walking down the tunnel in the Capitol, filming on Facebook Live, when Cori Bush screamed at me. (By the way, this is the same woman, now a member of Congress, who was the leader of the St. Louis BLM terrorist mob who trespassed into a gated neighborhood and led the dangerous mob by the home of Mark and Patricia McCloskey.[68] They had to defend their lives and their home holding their legally owned guns. Thank God they were gun owners!) After she passed by me, Cori Bush turned back. Her voice was so weirdly deep and aggressive that I thought it was a man as she repeatedly yelled, *"Follow the rules and put on a mask!"*

"Stop yelling at people! Stop being a hypocrite!" I said back to her. I turned around, ignored her, and kept walking in the opposite direction. I called her a hypocrite because she was voting to impeach President Trump for "inciting violence," and she led a violent mob that threatened to murder the McCloskeys and was now aggressively attacking me over unscientific and absurd mask rules imposed by Nancy Pelosi. After the incident, she went to Nancy Pelosi's office and claimed I had *attacked* her. She blatantly lied to the Speaker of the House and the press as she spread this fiction, saying she felt her life was in danger. She railed on, claiming I was a dangerous, insurrectionist, radical MAGA Republican. Of course, the press ran with it.

It's my word against hers, right? Well, what she didn't know was that I had the whole thing on *video*! Fox and a few others picked it up, but they'd already run the stories and don't retract these days. Cori Bush still got her office moved away from mine to one with a nicer view, and Pelosi needlessly provided her with an armed security detail, too. Pretty hypocritical that Cori Bush is always trying to ban Americans from owning guns, yet she is the one that leads the violent mobs and aggressively attacks people!

During COVID and now, I never backed down, and I never will. I introduced multiple pieces of legislation to help preserve our freedoms. In one, I sought to make vaccine and mask mandates illegal. I proposed removing liability protection from vaccine makers, allowing people to sue. And I introduced a bill on behalf of vaccine victims to investigate VAERS (Vaccine Adverse Events Reporting System), the CDC's self-reporting system for individuals, doctors, and hospitals.

There are over 1.5 million VAERS reports of vaccine injuries and over 35,000 deaths, which is far more than any other vaccine, yet it has never been investigated. The government funded these COVID vaccines and then mandated the vaccines on federal workers and contractors. Many city and state governments mandated the vaccines as well. If people refused to take the COVID vaccines, they were fired from their jobs or kicked out of the military, losing their ability to provide for themselves and their families. If the government uses the American taxpayers' hard-earned tax dollars to pay for the vaccines and then forces people to take them, how can it refuse to investigate over 1.5 million VAERS reports of vaccine injuries and 35,000 deaths? How dare they?

I want people to know how hard I'm fighting because someone must stand up for our freedoms in Congress. I have been relentlessly attacked, fined, and harassed—but it's worth it because I believe it's my job to fight for our freedom. It's my job, as well, to try to make sure that these abuses don't happen again because we've now seen the face of communism in America—and it's not only ugly, it's deadly. Let's look at the way communist ideology has entered our society under the guise of environmentalism.

10

No Green Deal

THE GREEN NEW DEAL SHOULD terrify every single American. It amazes me that people don't realize the magnitude of change this bill proposes. It's a communist manifesto and a radical change to our government. Most think the Green New Deal only addresses climate change and taking care of the earth by reducing greenhouse gas emissions, which sound like responsible things to do. The reality is these issues are smokescreens the bill uses to cover up profoundly unconstitutional changes to our very way of life. The Green New Deal is driven by some of the most extreme, America-last Democrats in our government.

I know this because I actually read the Green New Deal for the first time during my freshman year of Congress. The best thing any voter can ever do is read bills directly. I get paid to do this, but none of us can take anything for granted these days. The American people need to know exactly what is in the proposed legislation because the legacy media certainly isn't going to hold Democrats accountable. It's up to us!

I only read part of the bill and couldn't believe the communist manifesto that was in front of me. The next day, I saw Alexandria Ocasio-Cortez (AOC), who proposed the bill, on the House floor. I walked up to her and challenged her to a debate. I told her as a successful businesswoman, I wanted to debate her on her policies. She responded in a voice that sounded like a young teenage girl, with sentences filled with "like," plenty of hand gestures and eye-rolling. I explained she had no clue how to run a business and she shot back that she had been part of opening a restaurant. I told her that being on the wait staff on opening night does not qualify as any experience in what it takes to make a business successful. She ended up refusing to debate me, and it's a good thing she is a coward because I would humiliate her.

A thorough reading of the Green New Deal begins with a special report on global warming, blaming human activity as the dominant cause of climate change over the last hundred years.[69] It jumps right into detailing the so-called climate emergency, which features rising sea levels, increased wildfires, more severe storms, devastating drought, and all kinds of other things threatening human existence.

At no point does the report mention that climate has been changing throughout Earth's history or how the current levels of CO_2 compare to historical contexts that span millions of years (long before humans began using campfires to ward off sabretooth tigers).[70] In fact, one thing they don't tell you is that higher CO_2 is good for plants and will help us grow more food to feed more people. While I'm all for the responsible use of resources and conservation, I can easily find countermanding evidence about human-caused climate change that shows our planet's climate regularly changes over centuries. In short, if the climate is changing, it has yet to be proven that it is different from how Earth has changed over countless years.

Signing on to a bill means you endorse it and agree with it. When then-freshman AOC first proposed this legislation in the 116th Congress, some usual suspects jumped on board right away: Rashida Tlaib, Deb Haaland, and Ilhan Omar, among them. Others joined within weeks, and soon eighteen of the most radical Left representatives had offered their support. This number kept growing until 101[71] of her fellow Democrats signed on to co-sponsor this naive and idiotic piece of legislation. What was once mocked even within the Democrat party has steadily become the position of all Democrats. Each of them blame human activity for all the ills of the world and the supposed injustices in America. By co-sponsoring this bill, they're saying this climate crisis is so extreme that it warrants changing the laws of our land, which would affect energy, diet, immigration, and air travel. It would even go against the Constitution itself; in short, they want to rewrite America to fit AOC's communist fantasy.

But is human activity the dominant cause of climate change? We live on a ball of rock, water, and air that rotates as it circles a big, flaming ball of gas, the Sun. Our own galaxy is filled with planets, moons, and heavenly objects, all rotating and spinning, with gravity pulling on one another while moving throughout a universe that we don't even fully understand yet. With all that going on, anyone who thinks our climate is not going to change is a complete moron.

Throughout the ages, Earth has warmed and cooled. Some of it is related to our air. Taking CO_2 as an example, we're currently around 420 ppm (parts per million), up from a pre-industrial concentration of around 280 ppm but down from concentrations of 3000-9000 ppm millions of years ago when the earth was roughly ten degrees Celsius warmer than today.[72] Despite what you hear in the media, CO_2 isn't even the worst culprit among greenhouse gasses—for example, water vapor has a greater impact on temperature. No, the truth is that the composition of our atmosphere is just one small part of our climate, but a far bigger factor involves massive, complex systems in our Sun. Sunspots, changes in output, and other solar cycles go through regular changes that can be charted back countless years, dramatically affecting Earth's climate.

In short, while there is a measurable increase in CO2, it's impossible to lay all of climate change at the feet of humans. Earth has gone through hot periods and ice ages regularly throughout its history, and we've even had little rapid coolings and warmings in the recent past, like the Little Ice Age. (By the way, no one paid taxes to a past government to melt the ice during the ice age. Carbon lies are a money scam.) We are part of a much bigger system that has operated without us for eons and will continue to do so long after we're gone, regardless of dumb politicians' schemes.

Yet AOC and others want us to believe that humans alone are responsible for catastrophic climate change. And she wants us, especially in the United States, to take on an impossible financial burden to "stop" this process by deindustrializing back to pre-1800s levels. Say goodbye to air travel, internal combustion engines that allow us to farm and transport food, most forms of energy production to light and heat our homes . . . and hamburgers because too many cow farts will raise the temperature, melt the ice caps, and flood their beachfront properties.

The Democrats want us to believe the science is settled on global warming. Still, Senator Jim Inhofe, among others, made a point of noting that he talked to scientists who disagreed with their assessment in a document titled US Senate Committee on Environment & Public Works.[73] In it, Inhofe refutes twelve major claims made by climate alarmists. His document is but one of many such works that got swept under the table because it doesn't fit the narrative. Groups of other scientists have signed studies showing there is *no* consensus.

Here's the deal: the science isn't settled, and the rhetoric-laced takeover proposed by the Green New Deal and similar legislation is nothing more than a political power grab preying on the fears of the American people. It will remake America as we know it, turning us into a communist nation that puts the power in the hands of the (Democrat-run) government, all supposedly to save us from a climate catastrophe that doesn't exist. The Green New Deal is idiotic and insulting to anyone's intelligence. Yet, the Left has embraced it. Why? Because it's a path to more power, money, and influence for the Democrat party.

Inconvenient Facts

AOC and others cite the "science" that falls in their favor, just like Dr. Fauci and others did during COVID, but for every study proclaiming human-caused climate change, others are refuting it. Take, for instance, rising ocean levels. While they say sea levels are rapidly increasing, we know they have been since the end of the Little Ice Age in 1850 and have been on a rising trend since the end of the last full ice age. AOC preaches fear that these rising sea levels will cause great harm (and cost a great deal of money), but there's no proof that the rate is accelerating—or is linked to human activities.

AOC herself tried to backpedal on her claim that the world would end in twelve years (we're already down a few!) by saying that Republicans had taken her sarcasm and dry humor for facts. "You'd have to have the social intelligence of a sea sponge to think it's literal," she tweeted.[74] Yet, as Fox pointed out, 67 percent of

Democrats believed her twelve-year apocalyptic prophecy, and 48 percent bought into the idea of a climate crisis.[75]

I'm pretty sure that if Democrats were convinced by their rhetoric, they'd sell their expensive beach houses. I don't see that happening, and these climate alarmists are still buying up the oceanfront property! In fact, not long after announcing that Meta and Facebook would censor climate deniers, Mark Zuckerberg added another six hundred acres of Kauai, Hawaii, to his list of holdings.[76] A little research into Democrats with oceanfront property might show which of them is putting their money where their mouths are.

Then they talk about wildfires (which are not caused by Jewish space lasers, just saying). Yes, we've had a lot of wildfires, but these aren't a new phenomenon. California has had wildfire problems since at least the Big Blowup fires of 1910, but I can tell you what makes it worse: poor forestry. Forests need to be cleared every so often, and nature self-regulates by burning up all the little stuff in the occasional fire. When we stop that process but don't clean up the forest floors—especially the areas under the power lines—it all piles up until you get a massive wildfire. Poor forest management, which includes not permitting logging and thinning of trees, has an enormous impact on forest fires, but that's not sexy. It's also a knock against blue states like California, which has been run and mismanaged by Democrats for decades.

Smokey the Bear used to tell us, "Only you can prevent forest fires." Still, we have strayed from the ideas of personal responsibility, and we have a duty to take good care of our forest. Instead, we have embraced a theology of climate hysteria. Humans cause most wildfires, so maybe we need to get back to Smokey.[77] No one wants to talk about the corrupt California power companies that don't make important safety upgrades or the record number of homeless people burning debris on public lands.[78] No, it's all about climate change.

Climate alarmists like to talk about severe storms and how their cost continues to increase. There's some truth to this, but it might not be why you think. As inflation rises, so do the costs of the damages created by severe weather. Each year, they predict more major storms . . . but research shows that hurricanes making landfall have stayed pretty steady since 1878.[79] Not only that, but the intensity of the storms has also not increased, as the alarmists claim.[80]

Along with storms, they like to talk about drought, but the worst droughts we've ever seen in our country were back in the Dust Bowl era of the '30s. We've had droughts throughout Earth's history, but the human-generated CO2 the Left wants to blame happened *after* the catastrophic Dust Bowl, not before it.[81]

Of course, storms and droughts will be a problem; they have been for all human history! And, yes, they're getting more expensive. Talk to Joe Biden about actually lowering inflation, and then get back to me on a solution for that problem. The good news is, while fiscal costs have increased, the cost of human lives has not, despite rising populations. According to one researcher, deaths from extreme weather have plummeted 98.9 percent since the 1920s.[82]

The Immigration Argument Heats Up

I was utterly astounded that Democrats cited *climate change* as one reason to support their utter failure to secure our southern border. The Green New Deal focuses on the impact that a global increase in temperature of two degrees Celsius will cause floods, heat deaths, and mass migrations. Democrats can't seem to talk about climate change *without* bringing up migrants.

Climate changes aren't dispossessing people, and, as a major industrial nation, we do *not* shoulder the blame for climate change (and must thus ignore our immigration laws so these people can flood our country). Those ideas they spout are stupid. The truth is that immigrants are searching for paying *work* and a better life, or they're trying to slip into the US for darker reasons like drugs and sex trafficking. Most people are trying to leave their country's poverty and earn their money in dollars, which are still strong despite Joe Biden's best efforts. However, they send those dollars back to their home countries in South or Central America, among others. They may someday return home, made wealthier by earning American dollars for work Americans no longer want to do.

I have no problem with people wanting to better themselves or take care of their families, but there is a legal path, and they don't have to come over the border illegally. I do have a problem with the fact that they don't pay taxes to the US, yet Democrats want to put their healthcare and other necessities on the back of the American taxpayer. In addition, we give *billions* of dollars away in foreign aid, giving these countries the means to fix their supposedly climate-change-related problems that the Left says are driving their people to our shores.[83] This isn't fair to the American people. We don't deserve to be bled dry for people who won't pay their taxes or for those developing nations who just pocket the money.

AOC claims that more than 350 million more people will be exposed globally to deadly heat stress by 2050. But data shows that cold kills *far* more people than heat does. In fact, according to a Lancet study, *90 percent* of the deaths related to climate are from the *cold*, not the heat![84] The study stopped short of claiming that global warming would reduce deaths, but the science here is inarguable. Consider this: when it's warm, you can grow more food than you can when it's too cold. Fewer people will die of starvation if we can grow more food, further decreasing the deaths if the world warms.

I feel for the already-hot, poorer countries that suffer more in the heat, but in Congress, we aren't creating legislation for the world; we're doing what's best for America first. While it mentions things like a global reduction in greenhouse gasses, the changes the Green New Deal proposes won't stop other countries from doing what they're going to do.

They want to keep global temperatures from rising more than 1.5 degrees Celsius above pre-industrialized levels to avoid the most severe impacts of climate change.[85] Still, they can't control any other countries. It's like they think they're God and can regulate the earth's temperature. They believe they can do this by reducing CO2, which only accounts for a small percentage of global temperature, and they want to go to net zero by 2050. (Net zero is what they call it when reduced emissions can be balanced by technology that can pull carbon and other products from the air.) Let's look at these goals and their impact, especially the effects of trying to go net zero.

A Green New World

AOC blames climate change for more than $500 billion in lost annual economic output.[86] But it's their America-last policies which caused our manufacturers, factories, energy companies, oil and gas companies, and many more to either go overseas or fail under unfair trade practices. The climate's not at fault; it's the global economy that Washington, DC, has created and pushed America into that has cost us jobs and destroyed families, resulting in lost annual economic output.

They don't seem to care that China and others are competing with greater advantages over US businesses. This is partly due to their cheap labor but also partly due to their businesses and manufacturing practices. From strip mining that leaves the earth scarred and as barren as the moon to dumping huge amounts of trash in the oceans and pollutants in the air, these nations get by with things that we don't permit in our country. If we mine, we do so safely; if we pump out oil, it's done as cleanly as humanly possible. We are more responsible in every respect than nearly any other country in the world, so why do the Democrats try to throttle *America's* natural resources and production?

Other countries cannot match our ethical and environmental practices. All the sourced goods and materials we receive are far worse for the environment than if they were produced in America according to our environmentally friendly standards. In order to make batteries and motors for EVs, China's lithium mines destroy the surrounding area and dump trash in the ocean, killing the coral reefs mentioned in the Green New Deal. And that's just fine with AOC. The Democrats don't have a problem hurting the environment as long as it's done by another country—and they can virtue signal. It's both absurd and disingenuous.

The Green New Deal wants us to get our energy from unreliable wind and solar while trying to kill off oil, natural gas, and coal. As it heats up, elites like AOC can go inside to the air conditioning. Their idiotic policies will make energy so expensive that ordinary people will struggle to pay for it. Wind and solar are unreliable because the wind doesn't always blow, and the sun doesn't always shine. Additionally, batteries with the capacity to store excess energy needed to bridge the gaps are extremely expensive to buy and maintain. Even in a perfect little green world, it turns out you *still* need other energy sources to augment wind and solar. They don't understand the concept of clean coal, how abundant and useful natural gas is, that it takes oil to move energy around, and irrationally fear nuclear power. So, they try to stick us with unreliable power and over-taxed supplementation while simultaneously radically increasing demand. Not a great plan!

It turns out, solar and wind aren't even that green! Those batteries they need to store the power when it's dark and the wind isn't blowing are costly and difficult to make, and they'll wear out and need to be replaced repeatedly.[87] Solar panels are inefficient and require toxic chemicals, produce harmful gasses, and leave a lot of waste materials that must be cleaned up. Wind turbines murder birds, literally, so the people who get their Arbor Day Foundation wild bird gardens going and promote wind turbine power are killing their feathered little friends in droves. Not only that, but wind turbines aren't sustainable financially and don't generate enough power to be worth the investment.[88] The idea that these solutions are the future is laughable; we're simply not ready yet.

When they passed the infrastructure bill under Joe Biden's administration, the Democrats spent only a small percentage on our roads, power grid, and so forth—you know, actual infrastructure.[89] They spent the rest on other, random stuff like COVID handouts and Green New Deal initiatives. When we follow the money, we don't see investment into what America needs; we see it frittered away on ridiculous expenditures. Biden's bill provided $10 billion for a civilian climate corps, $20 billion to advance racial equality and environmental justice, and $175 billion for subsidies for electric vehicles, just to name a few.[90]

I am convinced Democrats don't know how money works, only how to spend it. Otherwise, they would understand that net zero global emissions by 2050 is a complete suicide pact. It's unrealistic and will destroy our economy. In a word, it's *impossible*. Net zero would return the world to the stone age.

Let's assume that electric vehicles are net zero (which they aren't and never will be because it produces emissions to build them). But, in the mind of the average Democrat climate alarmist, the EV is our savior. So, they say to themselves that if we simply made everything electric—powered by solar, which produces harmful waste during manufacturing, and wind, which is unreliable and kills birds—we could quit adding emissions and thus cool the world off and make everyone happy.

So, this means no more internal combustion engines, for which we have infrastructures worldwide for farming, manufacturing, transport, commuting, and all the rest. Never mind that they were making great strides in making combustion engines more efficient. I'm sorry, farmers; you can't use your expensive diesel tractor. You'll have to buy an insanely expensive electric one. Sorry, truck drivers; no more trans-continental transport. You'll have to buy an electric rig that can only go three hundred miles a day and costs much more than a normal semi. The same goes for every school bus, delivery vehicle, and daily commuter car—all must be electric. I guarantee they haven't considered the cost of replacing the *world's* internal combustion vehicles with battery-powered ones. And then we get to air travel. AOC thinks we can ban jet airplanes, and we'll all simply *walk* to Europe or Asia. In her own New Green Deal, she proposes an underwater high speed rail connecting the West Coast to Hawaii. Imagine how a tsunami would affect your arrival time on this train! Or we'll build electric airplanes, which have to lift heavy battery packs as well as people and freight can only travel a minimal distance, and will be considerably slower. But all of this is just transportation.

What about manufacturing? No one would be able to make any-thing because factories produce emissions along with products. And if they do produce products, they'll have to mess with complicated carbon exchange scams (scams that have made John Kerry and Al Gore rich for decades). How much electricity would it take to run all the powerful machines in the factories and manufacturing plants? To meet this net zero goal, the world would have to stop making things—anything!

And where does all this electricity come from? They want to increase demand dramatically, but their technology isn't up to the task of powering our current needs, let alone the extra required by going all-electric. Perhaps we could all have treadmills at home and use those to power our houses and cars?

The truth is that we could never cut emissions completely. It's totally impossible.[91] The only way to go net zero is to offset emis-sions through carbon removal and carbon markets. And these are schemes, pure and simple, to make money.[92]

While so-called "green energy" people say they want things like wind and solar, they don't because as soon as they get them, they complain about the problems with these sources. What they really want is *deindustrialization*. They don't desire modern life or advance-ment; they want us to return to the stone age, except they won't like it if we return to burning wood to keep warm. That would be an emission! So, you won't be able to cool your house because we won't be able to make enough electricity; you won't be able to heat your home because that would burn wood.

AOC and her friends will "save" the world—but destroy civilization.

The Rest of the World

So, just for a moment, let's live in the Democrat's fictional world where net zero is even possible for America. While numerous nations have made pledges that they, too, will go net zero, I can assure you that is very wishful thinking. China, which said it would be there by 2060, in just one year, has ramped up coal production by 9 percent in 2022 over their production in 2021 and is building six times more new coal plants than anyone else.[93] Crude oil production increased by 3 percent in the same period, and they're buying more oil and gas from Russia than ever before.

And they're spending next to nothing on going "green." Why? Because it's *stupid* and prohibitively expensive and inefficient. China and Russia and developing nations will continue to use fossil fuels because they work, and they're available for all the poorer people in this world who cannot afford to make the switch to electric (really, no one can; they'll just add it to the debt). When these other nations fail to embrace the Democrat's Green New Deal, it will be a slap in the face and make everything they *say* they're trying to do (save the planet by costing us trillions) pointless. It will drive America into the ground while enemies like China surge ahead.

It's like a political cartoon, with Joe Biden and President Xi of China standing at the edge of a cliff. Biden promises to be net zero by 2050, and Xi promises to be there by 2060.[94] Xi smiles as Biden jumps off the cliff first. They've sought the fall of America for all these years, but if we go for net zero, we're doing it to ourselves.

Who Pays?

We have talked about the cost of the Green New Deal a bit, but I want to drill down deeper into this because the fact is, even if we could trust the government to determine the world's climate and run every aspect of our lives, there is no way to pay for AOC's plan. This is a fantasy designed to destroy the economy of the United States and a communist manifesto, but more than anything else—the Green New Deal is financial suicide.

By some estimates, the Green New Deal will cost around *$93 trillion*[95] (America is over $32 trillion in debt and climbing, just for reference). Even the lower cost projections for AOC's plan put it at $51 trillion.[96] Bernie Sanders admitted that the universal healthcare proposed in the bill would cost between $20 and $40 trillion over ten years!

Let's put this in comparison: the tax revenue of the federal government in 2022 was "just" $4.9 trillion and is around $4 trillion most years, meaning the cost of the Green New Deal is roughly *twenty times* the tax revenue of our country!

The Green New Deal is nothing short of a scam! It's financially impossible, and the Left are disingenuous when claiming they want "green energy." There's no way to get to net zero without destroying the world as we know it and returning to the stone age. No country can afford this proposal. It's a way to grind America further into the dust, and perhaps one of the best examples of an America-last policy I can think of. Just like in real communist countries, the Green New Deal makes the rich get richer and the poor get poorer while destroying the middle class.

The more the government touches, the more it ruins. Look at healthcare in countries with single-payer systems, such as the UK.

Let's see how much people enjoy waiting on a list controlled by bureaucrats for cancer treatment or being unable to see a doctor when they need one, as they do in England! That's a perfect example: the government's healthcare sucks, and people must still pay for better care. Under that system, you'd better hope you're rich if you get sick because the government isn't going to save you!

The government isn't here to save us; it isn't supposed to right the wrongs of climate or remake social justice in the green Democrats' twisted perspective. They want the government to take over because it gives them more money and power. Consequences be damned.

The only people who will make out under the Green New Deal are those favored by the all-powerful government. Only the chosen energy sources, carbon traders, and government workers stand to gain. If you're in an industry they want to kill, look out—it doesn't matter how hard you work, they're going to destroy your business. Unless you're one of their protected classes or chosen industries, you're on the extinction list and the future welfare rolls.

Green Justice Warriors

While I may focus on the absurdity of how much the Green New Deal will cost, how impractical it is, and how unnecessary I believe it is, within AOC's signature proposal is a great deal that has *nothing* to do with energy, emissions, or going green. Somehow, they use climate as a guise for addressing "injustice" in the most communist way possible. They want the Green New Deal to counter systemic injustices. How does that affect the climate? In short, it doesn't. This, my dear reader, shows beyond doubt that the entire legislation is nothing more than a power grab for extreme Left Democrats full-on embracing communism.

They believe that it is the duty of the federal government not just to halt climate change and prevent global temperatures from rising, but to create millions of high-wage *union* jobs for all communities and workers (except for, obviously, the millions put out of work by pushing us away from efficient fossil fuels). How will the government create good and high-paying union jobs and encourage collective bargaining agreements to ensure prosperity and economic security for all people in the United States . . . other than by taking over?

Only in communist countries does the government create and control jobs, getting involved in union disputes and bargaining agreements. In the US, the free-market economy does that—and it has been the success story of the *world*. Remember, everyone wants to come here. Why? *Because the American experiment works!* Yet now, AOC wants us to be just like Russia or China. And, while the Soviet Union collapsed and true communism showed it doesn't work, AOC wants the United States of America to go the same failed route that hasn't worked for anyone else.

We already have a Bill of Rights, but the Green New Deal proposes a different bill of rights, making it the job of the federal government to control the climate, the jobs, and our lives.[97] This directly opposes the real Bill of Rights as the Tenth Amendment clearly states that the federal government only has the rights and powers delegated in the Constitution.[98] If it's not in the Constitution, it's not in the government's power. And nowhere in our Constitution does it say that our government can control the world's weather, create and control jobs, and all the rest that the Green New Deal proposes. Every right not spelled out in the Constitution belongs to the *people*, not the federal government, and we must fight to keep the government from taking over with AOC and her cronies in charge.

Our Founding Fathers were smart enough to understand that power will corrupt, so much of the genius of America, including the Constitution and the Bill of Rights, actually protects the people *from* our federal government! This is the complete opposite of what the Green New Deal proposes, by forcing us to eat healthy foods and making it the federal government's duty to control our climate, produce, community, and resiliency. It is not in our best interest to give our government the power to control the weather (if such a thing is even possible), force everyone to go vegan, provide for nature, and control our lives.

But then they go further: the Green New Deal says the role of the federal government is to promote justice and equality by stopping current, preventing future, and repairing historical oppression of indigenous peoples, communities of color, migrant communities, deindustrialized communities, depopulated communities, the poor, low-income workers, women, the elderly, the unhoused, homeless people, people with disabilities, and youth. In essence, this makes it the government's job to fix everything that's ever gone wrong (at taxpayers' expense) rather than giving us all an equal chance to determine our futures.

It has never been the government's job to make everything perfect, and it certainly isn't its job to get everyone to the same outcome. That is called communism, and it destroys personal initiative and lost the Cold War! In America, we strive to give everyone equal opportunity. What we make of that opportunity is up to *us* as individuals.

America was designed with the understanding that God created all of us equal. Race, gender, identity, economic status, and all the other identity politics keywords they like to use do not change our essential quality. Yet people like AOC think some should be brought down in order to make people who haven't even tried feel better.

When founded, America achieved levels of equality that most countries have never dreamed of. Today, in some Muslim countries like Afghanistan, women cannot get an education, work a job, drive a car, or even receive medical care![99] In some countries, children are used as slave labor, and sex trafficking runs rampant. Many are not governed by law but by dictators. In some places, being from another tribe is reason enough for genocide. The peaceful transition of power we experience in America is just a daydream in much of the world. Despite all America has done to make our country—and the rest of the world—a better place, short-sighted people like AOC and Joe Biden cannot understand the beauty of our system of government, and they take it for granted. They think communism and socialism will improve America, but these concepts have already failed and will only bring this great country down.

Creating real equality in America means putting everyone on equal footing to start, not guaranteeing everyone an equal outcome. It means everyone has a fair chance, and we make decisions that either take us toward success or away from it every day. We will either do the right thing or the wrong thing. As we live, we create natural consequences for ourselves and others with our choices. We accept that other things are beyond our control, such as the weather, disease, and earthquakes. For these, we trust in God—not the federal government! By expecting the federal government to solve all our problems for us, we give it power that will, most likely, be abused and only create inequality. The Founding Fathers were wise to limit government, and we're fools if we give it too much power and control.

The Democrats add language about eliminating inequality in all their recent legislation. This sounds great, but as they promote justice and equality based on identity politics, they create more inequality.

You see, if you are a white male, you don't qualify for help in their books, no matter how badly you need it. It's up to you to survive, achieve, and be successful on your own. But if you fall into any of the categories on their list, you can expect the federal government to come in and fix it for you and give you what others must work for.

And guess what happens when someone owes the federal government their livelihood, survival, and success? They become dependent, and this gives the government even more power. Yet people will voluntarily put themselves in this position of dependency on— rather than protection from—our federal government because many people don't understand how it's designed to work or the consequences of going down Biden, AOC, and Sanders' path.

With the Green New Deal and other pieces of legislation, such as the border bill, Democrats are trying to buy votes. They tell people that if they vote for them, they will ensure that the federal government takes care of them. But the logic is a lie because, in the name of justice and equality, they are wrapping the American people with chains no one else has been able to bear. They will saddle us with impossible debt, unmeetable expectations, and unrealistic goals. I firmly believe that if they even achieve part of what they say they want, it will quickly become all about the next crisis that we need the government to save us from.

Currently, the government cannot meet 100 percent of power demand with "clean," renewable, and zero-emission energy sources[100]—let alone in a future world that has gone all electric! It's impossible to meet the country's energy demands this way, and even if we could, as we have discussed, it isn't as green as they say it is. The American people should not have to pay for it!

Efficient fossil fuels powered the expansion of society as we began manufacturing things at larger levels and steadily headed west, but they would tear it all down. To picture the world AOC and the others want, we must go back in time to find an era before oil and natural gas, before the railroads connected the continent, and before the Industrial Revolution.

Out of Contact with Reality

Actress Alexandria Ocasio-Cortez doesn't understand how economics, manufacturing, farming, energy, or transportation actually work. She's never lived outside a big city and doesn't even understand how food gets on her table or why the lights turn on. Never forget AOC, or Sandy (which is her real name), as a freshman member of Congress, didn't even know what a garbage disposal was until she moved to Washington, DC. She doesn't think about how these things work; she just has a warm and fuzzy idea that everything should be clean, sustainable, and "green."

The people in rural America understand how much work and energy it takes to grow our food. They know how much the weather affects us far more intimately than Sandy ever will. They understand how the sun and rain impact the crops, and just like there aren't atheists in foxholes, I'd be willing to bet that nearly every farmer has looked up at the sky and said a prayer when things looked bad.

Knowing what we can and cannot control, with the stakes being the food we eat, tends to create thankfulness, faith, and reliance on God, our Creator, the One who tells the rains to fall on the just and the unjust alike. Sandy wants the government to be God and for everyone to believe in it, but history has taught us that this is utterly foolish.

Sandy and the Democrats who have signed onto the Green New Deal have made climate change their religion and government their

savior. They have faith in our government to change the global temperature and, despite countries like China, that we can somehow
get the rest of the world to buy into their extremism, too. What
she doesn't understand is that while in America, people like Sandy
have the luxury and privilege to consider these things, in most of the
world, people are just trying to *live* day-to-day.

Think that it's all been stopped because the Green New Deal
proposed by Sandy didn't go through? I'm afraid it's not that simple.
The Democrats have basically passed a good portion of the Green
New Deal in major bills during the 117th Congress instead of passing Sandy's original bill. So, even more terrifying than the original
legislation becoming reality is that much of this idiocy has already
gone through, thanks to Nancy Pelosi's help as Speaker of the House
and Joe Biden signing it into law one piece at a time. While the bill
itself may still bear Sandy's name, it's actually Joe Biden who is making the climate cult a reality in the US, not Sandy (who, I should
point out, didn't actually write it but instead put her name on the
product of a communist think tank).

The Green New Deal is the very opposite of how our
Constitution and the Bill of Rights established our country and the
role the Founding Fathers wanted for our government. They recognized that our rights come not from the government but from *God*,
but when you take Him out of the picture and make the government
your god, you're setting yourself up for a system that will make the
government overreach during COVID seem tame. If we let the federal government take over everything, like Sandy wants, we will find
ourselves living in *1984*, which is exactly what the Democrats want.

America will lose under the Green New Deal. We will lose freedoms, finances, and business, and we'll hand it all over to a bloated,
all-controlling federal government completely at odds with the

Founding Fathers' vision that made America the greatest country in the world. It gives every advantage to countries like China, on which we'd be dependent for our electric motors and other manufacturing. And even if we did all Sandy wants, it still wouldn't enable the government to control the world's weather, temperature, and climate. Having ruined our country, the earth would still be hot and cold and have storms and droughts.

Climate alarmists must not be allowed to run our country into the ground in the name of a false god that controls every aspect of our lives. The Democrats who signed on for this bill are either horribly naïve or see the potential for more power, and we need to put a stop to the lunacy before they're allowed to gut this once-great nation and send us back to being a pre-industrial society. I, for one, will not rest until the Green New Deal is defeated, and I urge you to contact your representatives to ensure we block Sandy and her pet project at every turn.

11

Right Versus Wrong

FOR THE FIRST TIME IN a long time, with Donald J. Trump, we had a man running for office who stood for what we believed in, who spoke like a regular person, and who championed America-first policies—policies that the Republican party had not stood for in years. This is the kind of leadership we need if we're going to fight the climate alarmists trying to use fear as a way of making money and taking over our country.

What I like to call corporate communism has aligned Washington and the big corporations to make the CEOs and bureaucrats a lot of money, all at the cost of the American taxpayer. They have sold out America's smaller businesses and forced them into unfair competition with China, India, and Mexico. One of the reasons the establishment opposed President Trump is that his policies didn't align with their corporate communism. For instance, Trump put tariffs on goods from China, which made a big difference. Trion Mills, who makes those real-deal blue jeans, shared how Trump's trade policies had started leveling the playing field as they sold their products, but they're just one business. Let me tell you about an entire industry so you can see our America-last trade agreements' impact on America.

In Dalton, Georgia, which is part of my district, we have some of the world's biggest flooring companies. At one point, these American-based companies dominated the carpet world and brought lots of money to Georgia. However, styles and tastes changed, and people began to shift away from carpets to hard flooring. The thing is, good hardwood flooring is expensive, so customers began gravitating to other products, such as vinyl plank flooring. This cost-effective option began to seriously eat away at the market share for carpet, but it also gave foreign companies a leg up.

Each Dalton-based flooring company told me the same thing—Trump's tariffs leveled the playing field and countered unfair advantages. Hard flooring, such as vinyl and laminate hardwood flooring, made in China doesn't have to follow the same standards as American products do. China does not have the same environmental laws we do, for one thing. They are allowed to use chemicals banned here in the United States by the EPA, and the chemicals they use are another reason (together with government-subsidized labor) why China can make products cheaper than we can in the United States.

As people shifted to hard flooring away from carpets, these foreign-made products gave international companies a significant price advantage over American-made products. In my district, Trump's changes were just beginning to negate the benefit of that Chinese flooring. So, the bottom line: Trump was helping Americans compete against China, and it was working.

Even the threat of tariffs changed things, and together with a few other regulatory reforms, we began to see companies expatriate back to America. Businesses that had gone overseas brought their money back to our banks,[101] investing more in our economy—and

taxes. Trump's tax cuts were massive for businesses and regular people alike, putting money back into corporate America that could be
used to develop new products, give their workers bonuses, increase
their salaries, and so forth, all fueling our economy. Companies
could reinvest in their businesses in order to grow, add new products and divisions, hire more workers, and again, all of that fueled
the economy. President Trump's tariffs, tax cuts, and savings plans
were fantastic for America, producing low unemployment and *record*
employment levels for minorities.

Additionally, the Trump administration's reform of death and
estate taxes began to tackle a problem destroying generational wealth.
Every hard-working small business owner, farmer, and other successful individual wants to hand down the fruit of their hard work
to their children, but Democrats don't like people independent of
the government. When the government gives you something, you
depend on it, giving them power over you.

Biden continually talks about raising taxes, and while he talks
about increasing them on the wealthiest people in America, really,
his tax plans will not just raise taxes for billionaires but will directly
hurt the middle class. Biden's policies punish the embattled middle
class, which is a terrible danger to our country. Democrats scream
about wealth inequality, but when you attack the middle class, you
create an environment where the extremely rich find loopholes for
keeping their money, and everyone else has to rely on government
handouts.

Estate taxes destroy generational wealth. Just think about it:
unless you are a wealthy farmer, if the owners die and leave it to their
children, they may be unable to afford the state taxes and must sell
the family farm. The same is true of small business owners; if the
children aren't wealthy enough to pay the estate taxes, the business

will collapse. We often only think about inheritance money, but these are genuine dangers to the middle class.

The real tragedy? This money has already been taxed! There shouldn't be any reason for people to pay taxes on it again when one generation transfers wealth to another. The consequences of these America-last policies are devastating! It rips the heart out of middle-class Americans' ability to be independent by destroying the generational transfer of small businesses, farms, and other forms of wealth.

Trump's reforms had begun to fix some of the issues destroying American businesses and wealth, and there were plans to make further improvements. Some of us in Congress still want to protect Americans' ability to pass on generational wealth. Unfortunately, you would be surprised how this America-first thinking is opposed, not just by the extreme Left, but by representatives you might not expect—globalist-thinking, corporate communists who have grown fat and wealthy on the backs of hard-working Americans.

A Leg Up or a Handout?

Let me task you: which option does more for America? Government handouts or putting money back into our economy to fuel growth, produce more tax revenue, and employ more (especially economically vulnerable) people? Hard choice, right?

Let's contrast the Trump administration with the record of Joe Biden, who is bought and paid for by China, which becomes more evident every day. There is no chance that this corrupt President would ever stand up to China and create policies that would threaten China's trade advantages. Biden's policies are consistently America-last, and he is quick to give people a handout. He seems dead set against giving American businesses or workers a leg up.

From the moment Joe Biden took office, using the blunt instrument of executive orders, Biden began either adding new regulations that strangled American businesses or cutting those that Trump had removed. Both played right into China's hands. As America hurts, China benefits.

China understood the war against America decades ago—it wouldn't be military, it would be an economic war. And thanks to people like Biden, they've nearly won. The Victorian economic sphere was the first step, and they used our greed against us to sell us cheap products built on the backs of poorly paid workers. But with their economic victory in the works, they have the money to go to the next page: military dominance. China is currently building its military at the fastest rate of any country in human history! It's not just their millions of soldiers. They are developing stealth fighter planes, a nuclear arsenal, and a massive navy, just to name a few.

When you are beating everybody with your economy, you're winning; that's why no one will want to go to war with China. They have a massive economy, sell us a ton of goods, and now they have a rapidly growing military. In short, they're what America *used to be* before corporate communists like Biden began to destroy us, not from the outside but from within. Washington, DC's corruption and America-last policies have taken us from the envy of the world to second place. How long will we hold second at the rate they are eroding our foundation, the forgotten Americans of the middle class?

Far-Left creatures like Biden believe in a world economy over an American economy. They are utterly committed to this ideal at the expense of our own country—a country they claim to love but show no evidence they actually support.

Not only that, but they're also ignorant. I'd love to know how many representatives and unelected bureaucrats in government have *ever* had to make payroll. They don't know what it's like to have *other people's* livelihoods depend on your ability to keep the business alive. While attorneys might do well in a courtroom, they may not make good politicians. They are risk-averse, and when you're scared of the future, you will always find a reason *not* to do something. They may have an expensive education, possibly a small career, and may be very smart, but they use their smarts to argue their way *out* of doing things.

A good business owner knows that you must always innovate and try new things to stay ahead of the competition. It's what drives the free-market economy and capitalism, and it's why this system is so beautiful. When you try new things, and they work, you succeed. Risk-averse politicians don't understand these concepts because they have not lived it.

I wish I were just talking about the Democrats, but this problem is true of the Republican party as well. In fact, I believe it's a fatal flaw with the Republican party; very smart Republicans may understand the law and come up with ideas, but they also are swift to come up with all the reasons they *cannot* defeat the Democrats. We're always on the defensive, and just like America, we're losing.

Let's look at who is beating us; first, you've got Biden himself. Anyone with a brain could see he was unfit for office as he campaigned from the safety of his basement—no one could see how much he'd declined. A far-Left Democrat posing as a moderate, the spineless and corrupt Joe Biden has repeatedly shown his true colors, such as betraying his stance against abortion, which once defined him as a Catholic. We'll spend a lot more time on Biden elsewhere in the book, so let's take a moment to look at some of the other Democrats gaining notoriety.

We've watched people like Cori Bush gain power. Remember, this is a woman who led the violent BLM mob through the St. Louis neighborhood of the McCloskeys, a pair of personal injury attorneys. During a season of violent riots where BLM rioters destroyed businesses, burned buildings, and shot police officers, the McCloskeys endured threats ranging from murder to rape to burning down their house. They opposed those threatening them by brandishing their firearms. Guilty of the unforgivable crime of standing up against the Left, as Mark McCloskey put it, they stood their ground. Meanwhile, Cori Bush led the mob through their private gated neighborhood with a megaphone, and now this woman is in Congress!

Or take the case of Maxine Waters and other older Democrats. This woman was a political activist who had held power way too long. Married to a wealthy banker in California, she sat as the chairwoman on the Financial Services Committee—yet it seems as if she understands *very little* about finances. This is the same woman who advocated more rioting and confrontation during the Derek Chauvin trial.[102] She demonstrated no understanding of the justice system and promoted harassing Trump supporters,[103] sounding the dog whistle for violence against Republican lawmakers and voters.

On the younger side of the Left, you have people like Ilhan Omar, who comes from Somalia and is a radical Muslim.[104] She aligns herself with the Muslim Brotherhood[105] and people like Linda Sarsour,[106] an extremely dangerous woman supported by the Southern Poverty Law Center who advocated *jihad* against Trump.[107] Ilhan Omar married her *brother*, breaking immigration laws to get him into the country,[108] and she somehow still managed to become a Congresswoman! She now uses her voice for antisemitism and supports jihad against Israel, our ally, by embracing groups like Hamas, a terrorist organization supported by Iran. Most of all, Ilhan Omar should be held accountable for sharing the bail bond link for the Minnesota Freedom Fund to bail out violent Antifa and BLM rioters during the riots in the summer of 2020. However, she wasn't the only one who encouraged people to donate money to bail out criminals who would go back to the streets to riot again. Our current Vice President of the United States of America, Kamala Harris, also shared the bail link, encouraging the destruction of communities and violent attacks against innocent Americans and police.

And, of course, we cannot forget AOC—Alexandria Ocasio-Cortez, an actress who basically tried out with a funded political group looking for a candidate for New York's 14th Congressional district. A liar, AOC grew up in a nice family, not the poor one she claims,[109] and has a degree from Boston University in international relations and economics. Briefly a bartender, this woman has zero life experience in anything. She's of course, a radical leftist, who has promoted communist ideals, while being aligned with Bernie Sanders. Having been elected thanks to the image and funding of her backers, she now proposes legislation like the Green New Deal.

While I attack Democrats, don't get me wrong; I attack Republicans too. I actually ran for Congress because I was furious that Republicans didn't act when they had the chance. Under President Trump, we had full control of the House and the Senate his first two years. Somehow, Republicans did not fund and build the wall, defund sanctuary cities, repeal Obamacare, or defund Planned Parenthood. That failure is what drove me to run for Congress. But we had four years of trying to fight the establishment and enact America-first policies. Imagine if this had been a full Republican party effort. I shake my head at that lost opportunity.

We enjoyed a term of actual world peace under Trump—peace through strength, something sorely lacking under Biden. Trump didn't just spend a lot on our military; he *invested* his time into them. By rebuilding America's military and not putting up with other countries' crap, he repositioned America as the world's superpower and a force no one wanted to mess with. I feel this understanding of the military came from his time in military school as a child and his great respect for our nation's heroes. He stood out from other presidents in how he went to military bases worldwide. He was known for visiting soldiers in Walter Reed and other hospitals; whenever they were injured, he would meet with them when he could and call their families. I'll never forget how he greeted the planes and coffins of America's sons and daughters when they came home. I understand that he greeted nearly every deceased service member when they returned home, something no other president has done—a tradition Biden immediately spurned.

Trump would never brag about those things himself, but I have seen it and talked to people who saw how he simply understood and sincerely loved the people of our military. He saw them as actual people, not numbers, and he respected their sacrifice when they were killed. It's like he was losing one of his family members! It wasn't just for TV; it was real, and some of the most touching moments never made it to a screen. But then again, they shouldn't have to.

With the contrast of Trump and Biden's records on foreign wars, I'd like to take a detailed look into the war in Ukraine. It isn't just a telling situation I firmly believe would not have happened under President Trump. It's the beginning of an indictment against one of the worst and most corrupt presidents in our nation's history.

12

Just Say "No" to Wars

IN SHARP CONTRAST WITH THE peace under President Trump, as I write this, Joe Biden's corruption and incompetence have us on the verge of nuclear war with Russia. Putin and others have warned of nuclear war, raised their threat levels, and postured repeatedly throughout the Ukrainian conflict. But I'm not sure how stable or rational Putin is or how credible his threats are. Does anyone *really* know? And with Russia's former president Medvedev chiming in on using nuclear weapons if Ukraine takes Russian territory, I feel we have a real threat of war.

For many Americans, Russia's invasion of Ukraine in February of 2022 was the first time they'd heard anything about a conflict between these two countries—at least for years. A little research shows that they've been fighting over the Donbas region in Ukraine, where many people speak Russian, since at least 2008. Russia would say it should be part of their country since they speak Russian and went on and on about Nazi militias in Ukraine as their rationale for invading.

Before the start of the war, the liberal media wrote about some Nazi groups, and the Ukrainian government—a historically corrupt body, which we'll get into later—had killed around 14,000 people in conflicts in the Donbas region. Reportedly, many of the people in this area want to be part of Russia, giving Putin a shred of legitimacy for his ambitions. In short, the Ukrainian conflict is not new, and neither of these countries has any moral high ground to stand on.

While Vladimir Putin may have claimed altruistic motives, he also had military and economic goals for the invasion. Putin wanted Russian ports in the Black Sea and access to the area's abundant natural resources, which are only growing in value because of our pressure to switch to EVs.

So, that's the stage, but it's also important to know the players. We obviously have Vladimir Putin, who is aggressive in his leadership and has justified the invasion. Then we have former comedian Volodymyr Zelenskyy in Ukraine—a man with a special friend, Joe Biden.

I serve on the House Oversight Committee, and our investigation into Joe Biden and his family's business deal has uncovered that the Biden family has been greatly enriched by Ukraine. This includes a $5 million bribe to then-Vice President Joe Biden and another $5 million to Hunter Biden from the oligarch who owns Burisma, a Ukrainian holding company with corrupt ties to Joe and Hunter Biden. Burisma is owned by a super-corrupt, wealthy man, Mykola Zlochevsky, who is now ratting on Joe Biden and his involvement in Hunter's business deals. During Joe Biden's terms as Vice President of the United States, Burisma paid Hunter Biden for a job for which he had no qualifications, except that his father was the Vice President of the United States of America. Joe, ironically tasked with investigating corruption as Vice President, was supposed to keep an eye on money going to highly corrupt Ukraine. Instead, his family got filthy rich on the US dollars going to Ukraine, thanks to Hunter's crooked business dealings with Burisma, Rosemont Seneca, and the many other shell companies.

And Joe Biden delivered. He is even on record. In a 2016 video, he brags about threatening to withhold $1 billion in USAID to Ukraine unless they fire Ukrainian Prosecutor General Viktor Shokin, who just so happened to be investigating Burisma.

During our investigation, we uncovered that the Bidens have a network of shell LLCs, through which they have laundered millions over the years. They've opened and closed dozens of LLCs, where they took payments from foreign countries and doled out payments to various family members.

Once decried as purely conspiracy theories—if the media reported on it at all—I have seen the many bank statements, thousands of pages of SARs (suspicious activity reports), and more that clearly show the connections between the Bidens and foreign governments such as Ukraine's. Tragically, we knew much of this *before* the 2020 election, and instead of being blocked and stonewalled, this information should have resulted in investigations and influenced American voters. Bill Barr, Attorney General under President Trump, was even in possession of an FBI 1023 unclassified form in June 2020 that was filled out by the FBI's top informant, who the FBI paid $200,000 for the information. It outlined the $5 million bribe to Joe Biden to make Burisma's "problems go away"[110] but they did not investigate or prosecute, let alone make the *unclassified* form available to the American people. Along with failures and cover-ups like this, many never heard about the incriminating information on Hunter Biden's laptop because of media bias, big tech censorship, and the weaponization of and coverups within the DOJ.

Crooked Bedfellows

What exactly does all this have to do with a war in Ukraine? Remember the little recording where Joe Biden bragged about threatening to withhold $1 *billion* in US support to Ukraine if they didn't fire a prosecutor? That prosecutor happened to be going after Hunter Biden for corruption while Volodymyr Zelenskyy was president of Ukraine, and lots of dirty business was going on through Hunter and Burisma. This is the same Volodymyr Zelenskyy who was on the other end of a noteworthy phone call with President Trump in 2019, where Trump demanded transparency regarding the Bidens and for which the Democrats tried to impeach Trump. It doesn't take a forensic accountant to connect the dots and see that the Biden family got rich from then-Vice President Joe Biden pulling political favors for Burisma and getting kickbacks from Ukraine while Zelenskyy was president.

And then Russia came knocking.

At first, Joe Biden denounced the invasion and said that the US would not get involved in a war in Ukraine—they're not part of NATO. But here's the problem: Joe Biden, President of the United States, is a puppet on a string. Thanks to that little bit of Hunter/Burisma dirt, he's on the hook to Volodymyr Zelenskyy and Ukraine.

Despite the sentiment in the news, Ukraine is not a nice country. They've shelled and bombed the Russian-speaking people of Donbas for years, murdering 14,000 of them and sending Nazi militia groups to kill them brutally. Ukraine is one of the most corrupt countries *in the entire world*, and they own a piece of Joe Biden. And while Biden initially said America wouldn't get involved, here we are, $75 billion[111] (and counting) of military aid and humanitarian relief later. Just consider that number for a moment—all given to a notoriously corrupt government, not even a part of NATO. This doesn't even include the $1 billion that America sends to Ukraine every single month to prop up their government. That money pays their politician's salaries and retirements and even keeps the lights on in their government buildings.

Given the history of Biden's "business deals" in Ukraine, you can imagine the conversation between Volodymyr Zelenskyy and Joe Biden and picture the words "You owe me" coming very heavily into the discussion.

We have no reason to be involved in Ukraine's war with Russia. That war doesn't affect America's interests, and we didn't get involved in previous strife over the Donbas region. Ukraine is not a country we're sworn to protect against Russian aggression. Yet, here we are, depleting our military reserves, sending Ukraine an unbelievable amount of money, and ratcheting tensions up to the point of nuclear war entering the conversation.

Many like the narrative of plucky Ukraine fighting back against the waves of Russian tanks with drones and guns. We've sent them countless weapons while completely ignoring our own border security and leaving it open to a daily invasion. We've seen assassination attempts against Putin, the destruction of the Nord Stream 2 pipeline, various targets within Russian-controlled areas blown up, and innocent people dying. The CIA and Biden's State Department may be engaged at unknown levels, which is disturbing considering we shouldn't even be involved.

I voted on the first resolution that came out directly after Russia invaded, and I condemned the war in Ukraine. But I have also voted against every single funding bill for Ukraine. Why? Because our country is $32 *trillion* in debt, and we cannot afford to fund a war, let alone be involved with it. Instead of financing the war, we should be brokering peace between these nations. Both Ukraine and Russia are rich in resources and produce much of the area's food.

Our Department of Defense's website states the DOD's mission is to "deter war and protect America's national security interests." Funding and fueling a war against nuclear-armed Russia in defense of Ukraine's border does not meet our Department of Defense's mission statement; instead, it completely undermines it.

This war has tragically killed Ukrainian civilians by the thousands and many thousands of Ukrainian and Russian soldiers. However, it has also greatly affected the world economy. Joe Biden likes to blame inflation on "Putin's war," but, thanks to Biden's failed economic policies, we were wracked with record inflation before the war. The war has made it worse because Ukraine was a breadbasket of Europe, and Russia is a top exporter of oil and gas. Biden overspent trillions on Green New Deal zero carbon scams and socialist initiatives in his first two years in office. Now, the effects of the war have only added to the problem, costing American families thousands per year due to record inflation while also affecting countless millions of other people around the globe. With more small businesses closing and credit card debt at an all-time high, those on the edge financially may be unable to hold on.

I voted against the sanctions set against Russia, not because I like Putin, but because they directly affected the cost of oil, gas, grain, and more for the entire world. Under Trump, we were a net exporter of energy, but Biden's America-last policies have made us dependent on foreign oil again, increasing the impact of these sanctions on our country.

My voting record doesn't necessarily echo that of other representatives. In Congress, we're constantly urged to vote one way or another. They will occasionally show us classified information to persuade us to vote a certain way, but I don't always trust the information presented. (Especially the classified briefings where the very information they are telling us is already being reported by the New York Times.) War is one of those things.

The treacherous military-industrial complex—the State Department, Pentagon, and manufacturers—exist to make war. That's their job. So, when the guys from the State Department and the CIA showed up with classified information to persuade the members of Congress to vote to fund Ukraine, I questioned some of the narrative.

The military-industrial complex gets too much out of conflict for us to ignore their motivations, and it's been easy to see how they would benefit from the war in Ukraine. They are often vilified in conservative circles, but I'm not against weapons manufacturers, the State Department, or the Pentagon. I want a strong military. However, I am absolutely against the military-industrial complex abusing the American people—both in the cost of lives and tax dollars—by waging foreign wars where America has no national security interests. Often, these wars cost many lives and countless dollars, but they make manufacturers a lot of money and let the Pentagon and State Department flex their muscles.

At the beginning of the conflict, the intelligence community told us constantly that Putin was just like Hitler, wanting to gobble up all of Europe. He's obviously not a choir boy, and he did invade a neighboring country, but I also don't see evidence of a continuing threat to Europe or NATO. Russia wanted the ports and resources in the Donbas, and Putin saw an opportunity to take them. If he could take the entire country and install a puppet government, all the better, he thought. But is there really a threat to Poland or Germany, or others?

The people in the intelligence community presenting us with this information were some of the same ones who said the Hunter Biden laptop wasn't real and was just a conspiracy theory. And we all know how accurate that turned out to be! It's not enough to look at the material you're presented; you also must look at the motives of those giving it to you. I openly question the military-industrial complex and everything they do.

They love a good regime change, and they want Putin out. He's powerful, ruthless, and loves oil and gas, which runs against the grain we're being forced toward with the Green New Deal-type policies in the West. Never forget, these foreign wars all come down to *money*, so let's look at how money works in the war in Ukraine.

It's All About the Money

The wars in which America has been involved in the Middle East—Iraq, Afghanistan, etc.—were about oil and, thus, money. However, the West is supposedly moving away from oil, and the big new money-making contracts are about "green" energy (it isn't really green, but we'll return to that later). Ukraine is wealthy and has natural gas and oil, but it has massive deposits of rare earth minerals, and that's what we need to focus on. Rare earth minerals are necessary for all the climate-hoax-promoting electrical architecture needed to shove us out of the age of oil and into the age of the battery. They're in your phone, your electric car, and microchips, which are everywhere these days. While we fought past wars over oil, the new frontier for foreign wars is over these coveted elements.

As I mentioned before, the Donbas region of Ukraine, and areas east of there, have massive deposits of rare earth minerals. Vladimir Putin says that he wants to annex this region under the guise of protecting Russian-speaking people and stopping the Ukrainian Nazis. If successful, he gets the ports they wanted and also gains access to these mineral deposits.

The Biden family has made a lot of money through corruption in energy businesses in Ukraine and China, and with the Democrats literally forcing the Green New Deal to transition us to dependence on batteries, they know exactly what resources will become more valuable. The new fight will be for these rare earth minerals, and interestingly, we do not talk enough about the incredible deposits Biden abandoned when we pulled out of Afghanistan. There was over a trillion dollars' worth of these elements there, but when Biden pulled out and abandoned Afghanistan to the Taliban, he also left these deposits behind. But why? Why would he do that?

I think it's because of China. Guess who controls those rare earth mines in Afghanistan now that the US has pulled out? China, which also controls Bagram Air Force Base. Joe Biden's treachery can't be overstated; he potentially handed over incredible wealth and a strategic base to China, undeniably our enemy.

But the malfeasance and treachery in Afghanistan go far beyond this. While trying to disarm the American people and destroy the Second Amendment, Joe Biden armed the Taliban terrorist government of Afghanistan, which we have fought since the early 2000s, with *billions* in military equipment! We're talking about countless guns, military vehicles, and even aircraft! (This is in addition to the nearly $20 billion in equipment we gave to the Afghan military during the almost two decades we've been there.)

The American people's taxes paid for the infrastructure in Afghanistan, from the roads to the buildings to the rare earth mineral mines. We built the air base, which was a pivotal and strategically important base that allowed us to better defend our military assets all around that region. And, at the cost of the lives spent fighting terrorists in Afghanistan over the decades as well as those unnecessarily lost in our botched pull-out, Biden abandoned Afghanistan and instead has us hemorrhaging more tax dollars in Ukraine. (Not to say anything of the cost to women and girls under the Taliban, and the fact that known terrorists are back in charge of the country.)

Ukraine—where Biden and his family have made tens of millions on shady deals and money laundering—is the frontier of a new war over the rare earth minerals needed for the Left's climate agenda. Ukraine, where we're pumping billions in humanitarian and military aid while we have no vested interest in their war with Russia, except to grind down Russia's military and weapons supplies.

When you peel back the layers of this conflict, you'll find that nothing is as cut and dried as it seems. For instance, take the Nord Stream 2 pipeline. Yes, the bombing impacted Russia, but it also affected Germany, which was buying Russia's natural gas. Germany is largely dependent on others for energy, so it hurt them a lot when the natural gas was cut off, opening the door to America offering our liquid natural gas in the European market.

So, on the surface, we're told we need to stop the evil Vladimir Putin from taking over Europe and destroying democracy. But then you discover the Biden family corruption in Ukraine, the rare earth mineral aspect, and America selling LNG, and it all comes back to money—massive amounts of money. It just gets dirtier and dirtier! War has often been this way. However, it's one thing to read about it in a history textbook—it's another matter entirely to have a sitting President of the United States engaging in this level of corruption right under our noses.

Right now, you're probably wondering what we're doing about it. I think it's tragic that the information about the Biden crime family's business dealings in Ukraine was known before the 2020 election, yet we as a country did nothing. Well, we're doing something *now* by investigating the Biden family finances, which we'll dive into shortly.

Peeling back these layers has also shown us all first-hand the level of corruption at the Department of Justice, the FBI, and other organizations that are supposed to provide everyone in America with the same standard of justice. We've seen there's one standard for most Americans, and there's another for the handful of ultra-elites, who can seemingly get away with anything. Joe Biden obviously thinks he's in this latter category, but I am proud to be part of a movement to show him he's mistaken.

In the coming chapters, we will look more at Joe Biden's corruption and that in the Deep State of our government. And, crucially, we'll see what's being done to address these problems and give all Americans equal justice under the law—"the Big Guy" Joe Biden included.

13

The Biden Crime Family

Joe Biden and his co-conspirators in the Deep State have gotten by with unbelievable corruption and crime for years, but the bill is coming due. A number of brave whistleblowers[112] and a lot of hard work have begun to shape up a case against the President for crimes stretching back to his days as Vice President, and I'm proud to be a part of the effort to hold him accountable.

Our duty on the Oversight Committee is to investigate potential crimes of waste, fraud, and abuse. We've been looking over 2,300 pages of SARs involving the Biden family since February of 2023 when Republicans, now holding power in the majority, started committee work. It's important to note that the Treasury Department isn't volunteering these reports, and we've only been able to view the reports for the names or LLCs we requested. There could be many, many more out there!

Produced from whistleblowers and research, the evidence is damning, and much of it originated with Hunter himself. Hunter's

WhatsApp records contained mob-boss-like messages like this one regarding China from 2017:[113]

> "I am sitting here with my father, and we would like to understand why the commitment made has not been fulfilled. Tell the director that I would like to resolve this now before it gets out of hand, and now means tonight. And, Z, if I get a call or text from anyone involved in this other than you, Zhang, or the chairman, I will make certain that between the man sitting next to me and every person he knows and my ability to forever hold a grudge that you will regret not following my direction. I am sitting here waiting for the call with my father."[113]

All along, Joe Biden has denied any involvement in his son's business dealings, but he has been lying through his teeth.[114] Hunter's laptop, which they tried so hard to discredit, was just the tip of the iceberg.

It may have begun with the Hunter Biden laptop, which has been unequivocally proven *not* to be a hoax.[115] Although it started with Hunter, it has led directly to President Joe Biden himself. As of this writing, we have spent months digging—beginning with the evidence on Hunter's laptop—through the Biden family's activities, bank reports in the Treasury Department, the web of shell LLCs, subpoenaed bank statements, and the connections with people, financial institutions, and foreign governments.

The trail leads straight to the "Big Guy" himself.

At the time of this writing, we are currently combining the work of the House Oversight Committee, where we've done the heavy lifting; the Ways and Means Committee, which deals with the IRS and the whistleblowers; and the Judiciary Committee, which has the FBI whistleblowers. Jamie Comer, the Chairman of the House Oversight Committee, must sign each subpoena we issue, but they come from the entire Oversight Committee. We've subpoenaed many SARs in the Treasury's custody filed by financial institutions from when Joe Biden was Vice President until today. And what we have learned shows us serious crimes that Joe Biden has committed . . . and for which no one has held him accountable.

The Treasury Department gave us *many* SARs, each comprising many pages. A SAR is created when banks identify suspicious financial transactions in their accounts. When they believe a crime may have been committed (based on the entities, types of bank accounts involved, and activity like wire transfers, transactions between countries, and unusual movement of money between accounts), they file these reports we're now accessing. These reports are simply staggering—but they're not just shocking because of the activities; it blows me away that we had this evidence for *years*, yet our justice system did absolutely *nothing*! It's not like the Treasury just "found" this information, yet no one did a thing! This is rampant corruption at the highest levels of our government.

For instance, I looked through pages and pages of SARs regarding human sex trafficking. Those aren't my words; that's what's on the report. Over and over, these reports establish the amount of money being paid to individuals, women's names, their addresses, their passport information, the origins of their passports (some from Russia, some from Ukraine, some from the US), even their phone numbers, dates of birth, and other details. This is very detailed information, and it paints the picture of what's called a ring of prostitution—a ring of sex trafficking that involves Hunter Biden. We have SARs detailing how Hunter Biden paid prostitutes and wrote off those payments on his taxes as business expenses. This came out with the

IRS whistleblowers because Wells Fargo identified them as potential human sex trafficking, yet the Treasury Department, the FBI, and the DOJ never did anything.

Other SARs describe money laundering, with wire transfers coming from China, Ukraine, Romania, other former Soviet Union countries, the Middle East, and African countries. In other words, it's a global network of shady business deals flagged as potential criminal activity, all tied to the Biden family. You'd think this would be all over the news if the legacy media had a shred of objectivity left. But they don't.

And here's the worst part: if it's a business in China, it comes with direct connections to the communist Chinese government, a nation hostile to the US. Their companies and banks are state-owned, so if the Bidens receive money from a Chinese entity, it's coming from an *enemy nation*. Many SARs from China don't show a company or bank name, meaning they've come from state-owned bank accounts affiliated with the Chinese government. Any lawful business would have a transfer associated with a legitimate bank in China. This means that our *sitting President* has received *millions* of dollars through dozens of LLCs owned by Hunter Biden, funneling a hostile regime's bribes directly into his pockets.[116]

In 2013, Hunter Biden accompanied Joe to China on Air Force Two, where the elder Biden met with Chinese officials. "The trip coincided with an enormous financial deal that Hunter Biden's firm, Rosemont Seneca, was arranging with the state-owned Bank of China," recounted Peter Schweizer in his book *Profiles in Corruption*.[117] Schweizer goes on to show that around ten days after this trip, Rosemont Seneca landed a deal with the Chinese government for an eventual *$1.5 billion!*[118]

Just stop and consider for a moment the impact of an enemy like China having its hands deep into Joe Biden's pockets! It would mean they have powerful influence over the President of our country, compromising him and the American people *completely*.

It's chilling—but almost less frightening than the fact that we had this evidence dating back before the election! Yet attempts to get the word out were stonewalled, and the justice system did nothing to hold Biden accountable for his actions.[119]

In 2016, Joe Biden was *on camera*[120] bragging about a conversation with then-Ukrainian President Petro Poroshenko:[121] "I said, 'You're not getting the billion.' 'I'm going to be leaving here in—' I think it was about six hours. I looked at them and said: 'I'm leaving in six hours. If the prosecutor is not fired, you're not getting the money.' Well, son of a bitch, he got fired."[122] Ukrainian officials revealed that this conversation was the result of pressure directly from then-Vice President Joe Biden himself.

And the prosecutor getting fired? Viktor Shokin, who was investigating none other than Burisma Holdings. According to documents on Congress.gov, Hunter's firm, Rosemont Seneca Partners, LLC, received regular transfers into one of its accounts—usually more than $166,000 a month—from Burisma from spring 2014 through fall 2015, during a period when Vice President Biden was the main US official dealing with Ukraine and its tense relations with Russia."[123]

Do I think maybe Shokin was getting too close to the truth? I sure do! Yet, close to the truth as he was, Joe Biden is so privileged that a recorded *confession* of quid pro quo was not enough to launch an investigation,[124] even before he squared off against Trump in a Presidential bid. This is still just the very tip of the corruption and criminal activity of Joe Biden.

The Money Trail

Serving on Oversight, I can tell you firsthand the GOP-led Oversight Committee staff and Republican members have been working very hard, subpoenaing bank records associated with the account numbers found in the SARs. We have many of the bank records and are matching the data we see in them with the SARs—at least for the individual and company names we know about. This is hard data, and it's all beginning to add up.

They tried to call the Hunter Biden laptop Russian disinformation, but this is no figment of our imagination. It's also not the same as the (now proven to be fake) Russian collusion idiocy the Democrats talked about every single day for years and yet had no evidence to support it. President Trump has faced trumped-up charge upon charge from a weaponized DOJ, all fabricated from shreds of lies that attempted to create a narrative of crimes. Crimes require evidence, which they haven't been able to produce. No one in history has probably been investigated as much as President Trump, yet he and his family business have passed muster time and time again. During that same time, no one has touched Biden. It is utterly unthinkable that we've sunk this low.

The Biden family's bank statements and the money trail of financial transactions tied to them is undeniable. There's no legitimate family business where they can show the products they produce or (legal) services they provide. They can't show us those things because they don't exist. The only thing we can find is the money—*millions* of dollars of it. There are bribes detailed in an unclassified FD-1023 form, including a $5 dollar bribe directly to then-Vice President Joe Biden from the oligarch who owns Burisma and millions from China, which have made the Bidens *very wealthy*.[125]

Joe Biden has a business, but it's not in real estate like the Trumps. It's in influence peddling and corruption.

Whistleblowers

As of this writing, the Oversight Committee is finally investigating and exposing the crimes that the Biden family has committed. And it's not just Hunter Biden, with his sex and drugs. It's not just Jim Biden, Joe's brother.[126]

No, it's not just the family—from day one, it's been about Joseph Robinette Biden Jr., President of the United States, and former VP. He's the "Big Guy" referenced in Hunter's emails and sits at the center of a web of astounding crimes. All roads lead to Joe, and we finally have the evidence.

We have proof thanks to, among others, a courageous whistleblower brought to us by Senator Chuck Grassley, who has his hands tied in the Senate. With Democrats in control of the Senate and Chuck Schumer in charge, they aren't going to subpoena any SARs, bank records, FBI investigations, or Department of Justice information. They'll continue to cover the Bidens and obstruct as they always have, so Senator Grassley brought the whistleblower, who feared for his life, to us in Oversight.

Senator Grassley has been working with this credible whistleblower for several years, and we're so glad he's finally spoken to us so we could subpoena these records. This is partly why winning the majority was so important, because now we hold the gavel with subpoena power in the Oversight and Judiciary Committees. In Oversight, Chairman Jamie Comer, with the full blessing and support from Speaker Kevin McCarthy, has been courageous enough to lead this investigation directly into Joe Biden himself; frankly, not all Republicans would be brave enough to do that, which is a whole other topic.

The evidence paints a portrait of bribes, favors, influence peddling, and extortion deals netting tens of millions. An email on Hunter's laptop breaks down the money given to "the Big Guy," Joe, as ten percent of a multi-million-dollar deal with CEFC, a Chinese energy conglomerate.[127] From that, we can assume that Joe Biden himself has been the recipient of a great deal of money thanks to these schemes as he abused his powerful positions in the United States government.

With each dollar, Joe Biden further compromised himself.

The Biden administration's Justice Department obstructed an investigation, despite the abundant evidence against him. Now, we also have whistleblowers from the IRS—Agents Gary Shapley and Joseph Ziegler—two brave and highly-regarded IRS agents who are testifying not just on the evidence against Joe Biden but also on the collusion within the justice system.[128] Despite Democrats trying to discredit their testimony, these agents have brought facts to light that are damning to Biden and his administration.

Attorney General Merrick Garland and Delaware US Attorney David Weiss could only point fingers at one another. Garland has been busy covering up the Biden family's crimes and, at the same time, failed to charge Hunter with writing off prostitution as a business expense and not paying his taxes.[129] Garland is in real trouble, and we're looking at an impeachment inquiry—I've already submitted articles.

The trail leads right to Joe Biden's door. The WhatsApp message I included at the beginning of this chapter, with Hunter saying his father was in the room with him, waiting for a reply, clearly shows that President Biden has been lying to us the whole time when he claimed not to know about Hunter's business dealings.

We have direct proof that Joe Biden is involved, both from Hunter's texts and from directly lining up SARs and bank records. All that's left is continuing to build out the web of fake LLCs, numerous bank accounts, wire transfers, and communications meant to confuse and obscure what our president has been up to.

We had an inkling of what was happening before, but now that we have an investigation by Ways and Means and Judiciary and the whistleblowers, the extent of the web of deceit is expanding. The sheer magnitude of the crimes here is shocking and has left various committee members speechless.

Completely Compromised

If the money was the extent of the corruption, it would be enough. But these crimes did more than make the Bidens rich; they've also compromised the safety of the United States of America. President Trump's first impeachment was for supposedly trying to urge Ukrainian leaders to fess up and report on the Bidens' crooked business dealings. We know that Joe and Hunter *did* have corrupt ties to Burisma; we already read his recorded confession.[130] So, how is this not enough to show everyone that Joe's ongoing influence peddling, extortion, and bribery schemes need not just to be investigated but have legal consequences?

He not only used his power to make himself and his family millions under the table; now, these other parties have dirt on him, which could be used in the future. We call that "blackmail." Joe Biden is compromised, and not just with corrupt oligarchs in

Ukraine but with China, which presents a genuine danger to the United States economically and militarily.

Hunter Biden's fund received *$1.5 billion* from China's communist government.[131] If the "Big Guy" received ten percent of that, it could be up to $150 million that China has put in Joe Biden's pocket. If someone has made you that kind of money and can dish on your dirty deals, they *own you.*

That means China, our enemy, *owns* the President of the United States.

How would this make Joe react in situations regarding China? It would make him incredibly vulnerable to blackmail! This isn't supposed to be able to happen to a member of our government, and we have laws intended to prevent it.

The same questions can be asked about Ukraine and many other nations (over the years, Hunter had over four hundred trips, possibly setting up more crooked deals we haven't traced yet).[132] How can Joe say no to Zelenskyy when we know that the Bidens have received millions from Ukrainian deals? He can't! Right now, we're funding the Ukrainian government, once the second most corrupt in Europe, with over $1 *billion* a *month*, paying salaries like Zelenskyy's and keeping their lights on. And that doesn't include the $113 billion, which is rising, that has funded the proxy war with Russia. Ukraine is not a NATO ally; we have no reason to be there. Except that Joe Biden *owes* them. Joe Biden being compromised means the entire United States of America is compromised, and we are hemorrhaging money to Ukraine because of Joe Biden's pay-to-play schemes. Joe Biden sold out the American people!

So far, he's gotten away with it, but no more! We have the evidence, and I will not rest until Joe Biden and the rest of his crime family are held accountable for selling out his country to make a buck!

The Fix Is In

How has he gotten away with this for so long? Here's my theory on why so many are willing to cover up his crimes: Joe Biden's crimes give many people in Washington leverage on him. They have dirt, as China does, and therefore they can *control* him.

It's job security for Christopher Wray, Merrick Garland, and many others. All you need to do is dangle a little dirt on Joe Biden, and you can look forward to a promotion. Maybe a piece of the pie? The Deep State has all the dirt on Biden, and they cover it up to keep their leverage. After all, he's the goose laying their golden eggs; they don't want him to get in trouble or the bucks to stop flowing!

Did you wonder why they put forth a tottering, confused old man for President? A man who campaigned from his basement?[133] Who sniffs kids like a creepy old pervert,[134] doesn't know where he is half the time,[135] and can't make it through a teleprompter speech without a gaffe or find his way off stage without being led by the hand?[136] A man who has to be told where to sit on cheat sheets[137] and gets irate like an Alzheimer's patient whenever he's questioned?[138]

Joe Biden is a puppet, doing whatever the Deep State wants him to do because they have all the dirt on his crooked dealings. We've wondered who is behind the scenes, pulling Joe Biden's strings, and now we have a much better idea—it's all the people who own pieces of Joe. He is the greatest controlled asset in the country, with Washington elites and the swamp (not to mention foreign entities like China) able to force him to do their bidding. They own "the Big Guy" in the White House and thereby control the United States through his idiotic policies and many executive orders. Controlling Joe Biden is the key to the White House, the US, and policy decisions worldwide. He's used like an intelligence asset, a tool.

And that's why they protect him. He's the best thing that's ever happened to them because all his crimes and corruption, and their cover-up, put them all in bed together to control the White House . . .
. . . and to devastate America.

This was the exact plan for Hillary Clinton. The Clintons also have a lot of skeletons in their closets, but we saw that even her classified emails, which would've landed someone else in jail, weren't enough to get her in trouble. She wasn't supposed to lose in 2016, yet Donald Trump upset their plan known as Operation Snow Globe. They'd shake the snow globe a little if she stepped out of line or didn't do what they wanted her to do. That's the same story for Biden, though they don't need to shake it very much because of his evident deterioration. Want a life-long, anti-abortion Catholic to cave on abortion?[139] Shake the snow globe. He's a thoroughly compromised man, and America is in more danger because of him.

They haven't turned on him because he gives them too much power. The media won't report on it unless the evidence is overwhelming, with a smoking gun that is completely undeniable. They still did nothing since we had that recording of Joe bragging about his quid pro quo. I know it will take such conclusive evidence no one can ignore.

This is one reason they're going after President Trump so strongly. They know he will clean up if he gets back in office, so they're using the Justice Department and weaponizing our legal system against him. We can't wait on Trump, though; like bloodhounds on the trail, the other representatives and I must keep on the scent, chasing down the Bidens and their crimes to bring justice back to America.

Justice in America

If people like Joe can get by with these crimes, we no longer have justice in America. We are seeing the results of an organized effort to take control away from the American people and law and order. The scales of justice have fallen off.

This is the real coup that started when President Trump took office and threatened the Deep State. We're seeing an operation that robs the American people of equal justice under the law, weaponizes the legal system against a political rival, and does everything it can to keep justice from happening to protect one of its own. The fix was in.

There is no justice in America because we have been taken over by a communist regime. This powerful and secretive party doesn't care about the American people and thinks only of holding and maintaining their power. They are actively destroying the dollar and burying us in debt. They're completely changing the way we use energy, trying to switch us from lifesaving, efficient fossil fuels to "green" energy that just doesn't work. They're exploiting the justice system to attack whomever they want and protect the guilty.

President Trump was never supposed to win; he was a four-year hiccup they didn't expect, and they're doing everything in their power to fix the game. They couldn't control him because he wasn't in on their corruption; he was an outsider. That meant the American people were free.

We can now see a trail of lies, deceit, and manipulation that has stolen elections, turned justice into a sham, and disenfranchised the American people. We're now compromised with a President who is a corrupt criminal, putting us in a dangerous situation.

The Deep State in control of our country and pulling Biden's strings are a godless, murdering group we must stop. They want to murder babies up until birth and would do it afterward if they could. They support genital mutilation, sexualization, and grooming of children, so they're also disgusting pedophiles. They want an open border and don't care about the drugs and cartels. They don't care about homelessness, unemployment, or the economy. They don't care about equality, women, minorities, or even going green. They only care about one thing.

Power.

We must *not* let them keep it! Empty liars like Nancy Pelosi, a godless woman who stands for so many evil things, must be stopped from continuing their agenda.

It's so vital you get out and vote. While people may doubt that the Republicans are doing anything, our work on the House committees is our best hope and a heavy responsibility. We have the best chance of holding these people accountable. We can only work effectively with the votes needed to investigate and impeach based on the findings we uncover.

Defund the Corrupt

Only a united and engaged Republican party stands a chance of gutting agencies like the FBI and DOJ of the rampant corruption in their leadership. Whistleblowers have come forward, exposing the need for purification, and we must fix it. We have tools like the Holman rule, which would allow Appropriations to take away someone's paycheck, effectively firing or impeaching them by taking their salary out of the budget. We can even defund entire departments if necessary!

Thanks to policy riders that determine how money can be spent, we can hit these people and groups where it hurts—financially. Right now, riders let us refuse to fund diversity, equity, and inclusion initiatives; that money can't be used in the military for mandated COVID vaccines; and federal funds cannot be used for transgender surgeries. All of which is happening now, but we can also write policy riders for the IRS, the DOJ, and the FBI, and we can use these riders to gut these agencies of corruption.

It's a lot of work—you would not believe how disorganized the flow charts of the federal government are! For example, you would think that the FBI pays every FBI agent, right? But that's not true, because some of the funding for the FBI is from the military. That funding comes from the National Defense authorization act, the NDAA, which means that if we are trying to defund the FBI, we must first understand how it gets its money.

I want to use the Holman rule on people like Jack Smith, the special counsel who is wrongfully prosecuting President Trump over classified documents. We could remove the line item with his salary and that of everyone who works in the special counsel.

This brings us back to how important it is for Republicans to win more seats; we need 218 votes in Congress across twelve separate appropriation bills to do this. We are currently working on balancing the budget, but appropriations releases the money to be spent. In the past, Congress didn't vote on separate appropriation bills; they used a trick to get members of Congress to vote for all the appropriation bills together in one big omnibus bill. We're not doing that, which allows us more control over how the money is released.

I supported Kevin McCarthy because he promised he would not do an omnibus bill, which creates manufactured pressure to get the 218 votes necessary to fund the government (which they always do right before Christmas) and avoid a shutdown. Instead, we have separate appropriation bills, which has not happened in a long time. Hopefully, this will give us the tools we need to use the Holman rule, rid the government of bad people, or rein in corrupt departments.

The policy riders I mentioned earlier will also be vital. In these appropriations, we can use riders to weed out the extremist Democrat agenda that wants to use federal money to fund transgender surgeries on kids and other idiocy.[140] Under the current Republican Congress, we won't have a repeat of the rampant waste from Joe Biden's infrastructure bill, of which only about ten percent really went to infrastructure! We can ensure that the dirty tricks in politics, which let them put so much pork into the spending, will not happen under our watch!

I wish we would've had a tool like the Holman rule to go after Bill Barr, who you'll remember had the 1023 form in hand on June 30, 2020, before the general election and did nothing with it,[141] except hand it off to U.S. Attorney David Weiss, who is now the Special Counsel supposedly investigating Hunter Biden. Weiss is just another corrupt attorney in the DOJ serving the interest of the intelligence community to keep protecting the Bidens. Just like Barr, Weiss had the 1023 form telling of the $5 million bribe to Joe Biden but did nothing with it. It is absolutely absurd to believe Weiss will fairly investigate and prosecute the Bidens. The media loves to say how David Weiss is a Trump-appointed US Attorney, but he was hand-picked by two Democrat Senators for the job. He will only continue to do what he has already done—abuse his power to cover up Biden family crimes, especially for the "Big Guy."

However, we won't let party lines or Special Counsels get in the way of defunding anyone responsible for covering up crimes! While we might not be able to control the DOJ and investigate and prosecute, we can surely cut their funding. It's a little like taking out Al Capone on tax evasion charges, but it's the best weapon we've got right now.

Accountability

We have a criminal in the White House because people did not do the right thing. Maybe they liked the access to power or feared that they could be implicated by association as well. Whatever the reason, they must be held accountable. The Republican Congress will do its best to use the tools available to do that, but I still adamantly believe that the power in the United States needs to reside with the *people*.

You, the voter, must share the responsibility by holding your elected officials accountable for their actions. If they will not tackle the hard votes and do what's right, we must replace them. We'll need to elect people with the guts to stand up against the Deep State and the network of corruption around Joe Biden.

Our country is out of control because no one has been held responsible for years, and look where it's gotten us. A deteriorating, corrupt criminal is in the Oval Office, Democrats are pushing an agenda of insanity that ranges from a manufactured climate crisis to a wide-open border to mutilating children, and our justice system is *broken*.

If we do not take our country back soon, I'm not sure how we will. We have a window in time, an opportunity, yet it will take bold leaders willing to make tough decisions. Our country's architects provided the tool for doing so—*if* my fellow representatives are brave enough to do their jobs.

14 ★

Impeachment Now

IMPEACHMENT IS THE TOOL THE Founding Fathers gave us to remove someone in government. Article II, Section 4 of the United States Constitution says: "The President, Vice President, and all civil Officers of the United States, shall be removed from Office on Impeachment for, and Conviction of, Treason, Bribery, or other high Crimes and Misdemeanors."

Impeachment starts with an impeachment inquiry, then an investigation, and finally results in articles of impeachment being filed in the House of Representatives that must be passed in the House with a simple majority of 218 votes. The charges then go to the Senate, which sits as the high court and holds a trial that concludes with a vote requiring two-thirds to convict the impeached official. As I write this, Republicans have a small margin in Congress, and I hope we can use this impeachment tool more successfully to address some of the failures in our government.

Some of these people deserve to be removed from office, and I think Joe Biden is at the head of the pack. I have repeatedly introduced impeachment articles against Biden for how he has failed the American people. Still, without a majority in the House, we didn't have the votes to move forward—until the 2022 elections.

I introduced my first articles of impeachment against Joe Biden on his first day in office, January 21, 2021, because of crimes that were already obvious to anyone not politically blind. We had the Hunter Biden laptop and another whistleblower, Tony Bobulinski, whose interview in 2020 with the FBI and detailed Biden-family connections with the communist Chinese government while Joe was still VP.[142]

With this and other information, I introduced articles of impeachment on the money laundering and pay-to-play schemes committed by Joe Biden. I also brought up Hunter Biden's involvement with Burisma, the energy company owned by a Ukrainian oligarch. This attempt to impeach Biden before he'd even begun as President was an affront to Democrats and got me kicked off my committees in retribution.

The impeachment articles read in part, "The resolution sets forth an article of impeachment stating that in his former role as Vice President, President Biden abused the power of that office through enabling bribery and other high crimes and misdemeanors by allowing his son, Hunter Biden, to influence the domestic policy of a foreign nation and accept benefits from foreign nationals in exchange for favors."

My charges were based on testimony from both Tony Bobulinski and evidence contained in Hunter Biden's laptop, where we have his text messages and emails.[143] A copy of this data was made available, so the press has it, the Democrats have it, and the FBI has the laptop itself. This is the same laptop that was disavowed as Russian disinformation, which fifty-one intelligence community members signed off on, including Anthony Blinken. It was a fake, they said—but in fact, it is not, and now has been verified as real.[144]

The articles of impeachment I filed were factual, and if we'd had a serious Congress, they would have taken those articles and conducted a full investigation. But as we all know, the swamp creatures aren't interested in justice but in power and preserving the status quo.

At that time, Nancy Pelosi was the Speaker of the House, and I was right over the target back then, which is why I faced such reprisal. I feel completely vindicated because, now that I've seen even *more* evidence as part of the Oversight Committee, I know how right I was back then. As we've seen, we have even more information now that implicates Joe Biden directly with financial payments, including a $5 million bribe he took from a foreign national in exchange for foreign policy decisions, as well as the many other items mentioned in the SARs.[145]

Abject Failure in Afghanistan

I also introduced another set of articles of impeachment against Joe Biden after his terrible Afghanistan withdrawal, which we touched on earlier. As commander-in-chief of our nation's military, they were his decisions that led to the failed withdrawal from Afghanistan. As a result, the withdrawal armed a terrorist Taliban government with billions of dollars worth of abandoned military weapons and equipment, lost Bagram Air Force Base and all the infrastructure we funded and built for Afghanistan's $1 trillion worth of rare earth mineral mines,[146] created mortal danger for our allies in the country, and, most importantly, led to preventable deaths of US servicepeople. It's unconscionable that we left so much on the ground, arming an enemy with taxpayer-funded equipment simply because we were in too much of a hurry, but it gets even worse.

Joe Biden caused the death of thirteen soldiers in a suicide bombing *we knew was going to happen*. Congress was briefed in a classified meeting days before it happened, informing us that they had intelligence that there would be a suicide bomber *at that very gate*! They also told the media, yet, despite the credible threat, no one implemented additional precautions. Thirteen of our brave men and women died that day, with others suffering serious injuries. Afghans were killed and injured as well. We could've addressed this threat, but we did not.

The loss of Bagram Air Force Base alone is such a tragic failure that it should have consequences. This air base was vital and strategic in the area, allowing our military to fly more direct routes and reach other locations and bases faster. Without Bagram Air Base, it now takes extra hours, requires much more fuel, and makes logistics far more difficult throughout the Middle East. When you look at the sheer monetary investment into Bagram, this is an even more galling loss.

However, there's a whole other dynamic; because of our rushed, failed withdrawal from Afghanistan, an enemy now has control of Bagram Air Base and all the infrastructure we built over the years—China.[147] China made a deal with the terrorist Taliban government that took over when we pulled out, and the Afghan government instantly collapsed. China, which has its hand in Biden's pocket, now controls Afghanistan's rare earth mineral mines, the roads we built, the facilities—all of it. While bungling the pull-out in Afghanistan, President Biden was simultaneously implementing Green New Deal policies that made us more invested in the electric vehicles that require those rare earth minerals.

I am not a supporter of these foreign wars, which our own State Department and the military-industrial complex have gotten us into. However, we'd invested unimaginable amounts of money in Afghanistan. We'd spent decades trying to help them establish a stable government, build their infrastructure, and change how women and girls are treated so they have access to healthcare and education. Unilaterally pulling out as we did caused a power vacuum the Taliban were quick to fill, rolling over the Afghan government with little resistance. Now, all the time and money we put into building up that country is lost, and the mining rights we could've used were handed on a platter to our enemy, China.

The commander-in-chief failed the American people and the entire region, and that's a reason for impeachment on its own. That's without saying anything of his compromised loyalties with China from his corrupt money laundering schemes.

Disaster on the Southern Border

I introduced another set of articles of impeachment against Joe Biden because of the disastrous situation his open-border policy created. These articles were based on the grounds that Biden's violations of immigration law caused a national security crisis on our southern border.[148] It would be shocking if I didn't already expect a creature of the far Left, like Biden, to pursue an open border. Despite all the evidence of the drugs, crime, and dependents illegally crossing our southern border, Biden refuses to change course or protect our country from these threats.

Greg Abbott, the governor of Texas, agrees with me that Biden's utter failure to protect our nation is an impeachable offense. Texas and other border states bear the greatest burden of Biden's dereliction of duty, with much of the deadly fentanyl and other drugs entering the United States from Mexico. Over three hundred Americans are murdered by fentanyl daily; it's now intentionally laced into the marijuana, narcotics, and cocaine infiltrating our country. An ever-growing pile of bodies lay at Joe Biden's feet because he refuses to do anything to stop this deadly tide of drugs.

Biden is aiding and abetting the Mexican criminal cartels' drug runners. Imagine the uproar if three hundred people died daily in plane crashes; we'd ground every airplane in America until we solved the problem. Yet, along our southern border, the crisis is allowed to continue because of the Left's liberal ideology.

Drive through any big city, especially the blue ones, and look at the sickening results of people hooked on fentanyl-laced drugs. In addition to the deaths, the drug addicts hooked on these potent chemicals look like zombies! I see them whenever I go to New York, Washington, DC, Los Angeles, or any other Democrat-run city. Thousands a day suffer the consequences of the illegal drugs that flow over the border. Still, the media typically don't say a word because they share Biden's political views.

When he came into office, Biden quickly repealed nearly all of President Trump's border security measures, gutting Trump's executive orders protecting America.[149] With Trump, we had the best border security in decades, but it quickly dissolved into chaos under Biden. Apart from Title 42, Biden canceled Trump's policies, such as the Remain in Mexico policy, and he halted construction of the border wall—a wall, I might point out, prominent Democrats only began to oppose once Trump was for it.

Biden also stopped maintenance of the border wall, including the many gates Border Patrol agents need for quick access, thus putting their lives in danger. Now, many gates are either stuck open or closed, both of which are problems, and the Biden administration refuses to repair them. This puts our agents' lives in danger and increases the threat to illegals trying to enter. If they get into a life-threatening situation and the gates cannot be opened, Border Patrol must take precious time going around. To keep them secure, gates that are stuck open now require additional human resources, which are always stretched thin along the border. One of the most frustrating aspects of all this is the materials to continue construction and maintain the wall are just *sitting there*, rusting and rotting in the dirt; the American taxpayer is still *paying* for the wall, even though Biden stopped the work orders.

Once again, large groups pour people illegally into our country. While we still try to strain out the terrorists who want to come into America directly from their hostile nations, we now have a porous border to the south that allows the very types of people who precipitated 9/11 to enter our country—along with anyone else.

We have immigration laws for a reason: to keep our country safe while still allowing *legal* immigration. There's a path for people who want to come into our country the right way, and every single nation on this planet has immigration laws for the same reason we do. It's insane to go against the laws of our country for the current political ideology of the Left, and it puts the people of our country at greater risk from violence, drugs, and crimes committed by illegals every day.

So, how does the Left justify their position on open borders in the face of all of this? It looks like fuzzy-headed thinking, where they're so "compassionate" to the people who want to come into the US that they just can't turn them away. They recently justified their beliefs in hearings where we grilled Secretary Mayorkas over the border crisis. In over seventeen hours in the Homeland Committee, we listened to Democrats introduce amendment after amendment, attempting to remove the wall from the border bill and give illegals ("migrants," as they call them) more money and services. Who needs to be a citizen when you can get this kind of handout as an illegal immigrant?

The Democrats unconsciously talk out of both sides of their mouths. While giving lip service about border security, they argue that we should treat the people sneaking over our border illegally better than our taxpayers!

They're such hypocrites! They all believe in walls; I know they do because they live behind them. They also have men with guns who protect them. Democrats love walls so much that they erected one around the Capitol when they felt threatened by an invisible QAnon army. Yet, while they enjoy the protection of these things, they oppose protecting the American people from the dangers in the same way. "Walls and guards with guns for me, but not for thee!"

Climate Change? Really?

And how did they rationalize the lack of border security? They defended their hypocrisy by saying that we need to let everyone into our country whenever they want because of—wait for it—*climate change.* Because of the "horrific" conditions climate change is supposedly causing worldwide, we're supposed to disregard all our immigration laws. This doesn't even make sense according to their own reasoning! If climate change is such a terrible problem, we're experiencing it in America, too.

I told them it was a lie to their faces because America shares the same global weather as the rest of the world. In America, we have annual hurricanes, tornadoes, high summer heat, chilly winter cold, drought, and torrential rains. Does our climate change not make our country too dangerous for illegal immigrants supposedly escaping their own country's climate change? Especially when these same illegal immigrants are forced to sleep out in the dangerous climate, literally in the city streets like in New York!

I reminded them of the incredible amounts of money our country gives other nations in foreign aid—money that could go to helping their people deal with this supposed climate emergency. Instead, it goes into some bureaucrat's pocket so he can provide Joe Biden with kickbacks. They all looked at me with the stupidest blank expressions, but I shouldn't expect anything different. After all, these are the same people who want stricter gun control in America under the rationale that it will limit the guns being sold to the cartels (which they're allowing free access to our country with their idiotic destruction of our border security). To the Left, it makes *perfect* sense to ban assault weapons two hundred miles away from the border in order to cut down on the *cartels* getting guns. They're fine with the idea of taking the guns out of the hands of the people they're putting in danger by stopping the wall and pursuing open borders.

But really, the truth is that it comes down to *power*—Democrats want more control, and people who are beholden to them give them power. Also, Latino voters typically have voted Democrat in the past (this shows signs of changing as the Democrats go even more extreme, alienating family-oriented voters). So, the real reason Democrats want open borders is to have more people hooked on free stuff who will vote for them.

We recently had to defeat a measure that would give illegal aliens the right to vote in Washington, DC. Can you fathom that? It's their mission to gain power and control by flooding the country with illegal aliens and giving them the right to vote. They even have T-shirts! "Hey, Joe Biden helped you come into America!"

Our safety, security, and even our *lives* are sacrificed as they gather more power. And it's not just the safety of our citizens; we can't account for half of the unaccompanied minors who have entered the US under Joe Biden's administration. We don't know where they are, and while we were talking about child labor in countries like China a few years ago, we now must look seriously at what is happening to these kids who are being forced into slavery in United States labor camps. "President Trump put them in cages," AOC once cried while wearing her ridiculous white suit. Well, the party of AOC and Biden has *lost* half the kids who've come in, and they don't know what's happening to them. As I write this, the Biden administration has lost nearly 100,000 unaccompanied minors while America holds the evil title of number one in human trafficking.[150] It's unthinkable!

Democrats don't care about the safety of these kids—or yours. They know they're going so far Left they're alienating voters, so they need to find more. They know that if all the potential voters in America got involved with the direction of our country, we could defeat the communist Democrat agenda. Many of our most conservative voters in America are passively on the sidelines. We desperately need them to stand up for the values that made our country great so we can close our borders and protect our people.

Following the Money Trail

Fast forward a little, and we now have information from the FBI's top-paid informant; proof of a direct exchange of money when a foreign national paid Joe Biden for policy decisions as Vice President of the United States. These pay-to-play, quid pro quo arrangements are grave crimes committed by then-Vice President Joe Biden, high crimes and misdemeanors—all criminal acts and impeachable offenses. Perhaps even treasonous, as it pertains to Ukraine.

As I now serve on the Oversight Committee, our committee members and staff, led by our Chairman, Congressman James Comer, have done incredible work investigating and uncovering the crimes of Joe Biden, proving I was absolutely correct on my first set of articles of impeachment introduced on Joe Biden's first day in office. No wonder Nancy Pelosi kicked me off committees less than two weeks later; I was directly over the target.

The FBI has proof of actual financial transactions where the then-Vice President got paid to make key policy decisions on behalf of a foreign national and a hostile nation. Yet, they have done *nothing* with it, which is why we had to subpoena Christopher Wray, director of the FBI. With the help of a brave whistleblower in the FBI, who came to our Oversight Committee through Senator Chuck Grassley, we discovered an unclassified FD-1023 form in the FBI's possession. It detailed then-Vice President Joe Biden taking a $5 million bribe from oil and gas businessman Mykola Zlochelvsky, who owns Burisma Holdings and Brociti Investments Limited, a Cyprus-based company. The unclassified form was dated June 30, 2020, and contained information about a bribe paid to Joe Biden in exchange for making Zlochelvsky's "problems go away,"[151] as he said it, in the form of getting the Ukrainian prosecutor Viktor Shokin fired while investigating Burisma for corruption. The form also contained information that Hunter Biden was paid $5 million—"$5 million to one Biden, and $5 million to another," as Zlochevsky put it.[152] He also said he had proof of the bribes in seventeen audio recordings, fifteen of Hunter and two of Joe Biden himself.[153]

Just imagine if Christopher Wray and Bill Barr had prosecuted Joe Biden for taking bribes in exchange for foreign policy decisions back in the summer of 2020 before the presidential election. Not only would they have done their jobs correctly, but they would also have saved America from this corrupt criminal who is systematically destroying America.

But they did *nothing*. This evidence was filed away and is undoubtedly being used to make sure Joe Biden stays in line or, rather, does the Deep State's bidding, acting as a puppet president and their intelligence asset. Instead, our Republican-controlled Oversight Committee has read hundreds of SARs in the Treasury Department and subpoenaed over a dozen banks for statements containing proof of millions of dollars in wire transfers from scores of foreign countries, including Ukraine and China. We're looking into fake LLCs and direct payments made to all kinds of Biden family bank accounts.

Detailed on the 1023 form, the Ukrainian Oligarch Zlochelvsky told the FBI informant that it would take us ten years to find it all. Our Oversight Committee has uncovered a lot of it in less than eight months, and we are still on the hunt. But it shouldn't have been this way, and Christopher Wray did not cooperate with us. Instead, he forced us to read a redacted version of the *unclassified* 1023 form in a SCIF (Sensitive Compartmented Information Facility, an ultra-secure room for classified information) in the Capitol. He would not leave us with a copy. It was a slap in the face and defiant behavior by the FBI Director, but what else would you expect from a man protecting his boss, the President of the United States (or rather his communist dictator, the head of the regime)?

Christopher Wray gets paid, from the American people's hard-earned tax dollars, to direct the FBI as it investigates crimes. He swore an oath of office, to which he has a duty and responsibility.

The same goes for Attorney General Merrick Garland, who, as the head of the Department of Justice, also gets paid by American taxpayers to prosecute crimes. Neither of them has done anything to hold Joe Biden accountable, and both were aware of these crimes.

In my opinion, this corruption of our justice system may be the most devastating part of this situation. We'll always have corruption on some level because of the nature of human beings. Still, when people of power like Wray and Garland do not do their jobs and refuse to prosecute the corrupt elites of our country, we have lost something good that had historically been at the very heart of America—the impartiality of our justice system.

It's heartbreaking to me that we had evidence against Biden during the Trump administration. While Trump himself didn't know and had no evidence of these crimes, people in his administration did—and they did nothing about it, either. If Joe Biden had been held accountable for his crimes, he could've been prosecuted under the Trump administration when we had a majority in Congress. He would never have been elected president.

There is a long list of consequences for America because this unfit, corrupt man entered office. The wide-open borders Biden enacted let in countless illegal immigrants, and along with them came drugs and crime. Three hundred people die every single day from fentanyl-laced drugs coming up from our porous southern border, killing men, women, and children. Our economy, booming under Trump, stumbled to a halt, and has suffered the worst inflation in decades, leading to the small-business-killing recession that has heavily impacted the middle class. We're on the brink of World War III with nuclear-powered Russia and have poured over $113 billion into funding a war in Ukraine and $1 billion every month to fund the government of Ukraine, a corrupt government not part of our strategic interests, while we're over $32 trillion in debt. As Joe Biden supports the war in Ukraine, we've driven Russia into the arms of other countries who are trading in their currencies, no longer in the US dollar. Now, we're on the verge of losing the dollar as the world's currency. Crime is out of control, especially in blue cities, and our children are two years behind due to shuttered schools during COVID shutdowns. They are under attack by trans activists who want to amputate their body parts and mutilate them under an evil lie about gender.

These consequences should never have happened—and would not have—had the FBI and DOJ had done their JOBS and prosecuted Joe Biden and Hunter Biden for their extensive crimes. This is another example of America-last policies and practices where the American people pay the price. The rich elites get richer on the backs of the taxpayers, seemingly exempt from equal justice under the law, while selling out Americans and their businesses under the banner of globalist economics and rampant graft.

If you or I committed the same crimes Joe Biden is guilty of, we would be prosecuted. The types of SARs we have on Biden would spawn investigations, convictions, and jail time. Look at how they used witch hunts to crucify Trump supporters or the January 6 rioters. Jacob Chansley, the so-called QAnon Shaman, is on video walking through the Capitol, escorted by Capitol Police. He was respectful, prayed with them, and told others not to damage property and to listen to the officers. Jacob became the face of the so-called January 6 "insurrection," and he was charged, prosecuted, and put in jail. He'll likely be off probation before Joe Biden, who is actually guilty of crimes, will even be charged.

But he *will* be held accountable. I believe these crimes will result in Joe Biden's impeachment, and we have so much evidence!

If Republicans do not vote for impeachment, I'll tell you right now that they don't deserve power. The evidence is clear and overwhelming, and if we cannot get a conviction, I will be ashamed of my fellow representatives.

Look at what past presidents have done to get impeached. Bill Clinton lied to Congress about a blowjob.[154] They came after Nixon, but he did the honorable thing and resigned.[155] Trump was impeached for a completely legitimate phone call with President Zelenskyy of Ukraine, attempting to investigate the extent of Joe Biden's crimes in that country, and then again for a riot on January 6 he did everything he could to avert, even asking for 10,000 National Guardsman to be at the Capitol on January 6.

There's no comparison between the evidence against Clinton and Trump and what we have against Biden and his family. We have so much data, from SARs to subpoenaed documents, as well as a serious whistleblower with high credibility. This man is not a novice; he has a great deal of knowledge about the situation—and is afraid for his life. That mere fact should terrify everyone; he's afraid of the repercussions of truthfully disclosing evidence of crimes against a political elite.

The DOJ already stonewalls or slow-walks cases. Hunter Biden tried to take a plea deal and plead guilty to tax and gun violations. At the same time, the Democrats patted themselves on the back that "justice was served." Special Prosecutor Jack Smith is hailed as a Democrat hero for leading another fake prosecution against President Trump for storing documents that he was allowed to have under the Presidential Records Act and continuing to investigate President Trump's alleged crime of caring about election fraud in the 2020 presidential election.

We cannot let this continue. It's time to fire them all!

Hold Government Accountable

In any business, if an employee isn't doing their job, it's time to let them go. People get fired for various reasons, from not doing their jobs to lying and stealing. Sometimes, people get laid off because the company gets too big, and they must reduce their workforce.

In government, that firing process happens to be called impeachment, and we use it rarely. But we shouldn't—we should use it as often as necessary. When these people defy their oaths of office and abandon their duties, we must fire them. It's time to use impeachment to correct our government's bloated state; we must cut overhead. But we especially need to cut the underperforming people in their positions of power and those who are corrupt!

We should run our government like a business because our government is currently the most mismanaged entity in the world. Our government takes in tax revenue like a business. Like any business, it has employees, properties, assets, liabilities, and bills. It's time we started running the federal government like a profitable business that serves its paying customers—the American people.

In a business, if you don't do your job well, you get fired, but no one ever seems to face the consequences of poor job performance in the government. The government never seems to cut a program or close a department; nothing ever ends, and it exists to protect itself and the people within it. They do everything they can to ensure their jobs never go away, no matter how poor their performance is.

But elected officials and government bureaucrats *work for the American people*. If they aren't doing a good job, we can fire them. Impeachment is the tool the Founding Fathers gave us, and it's how you fire people who have become corrupt, broken the law, or are failing our country, and I think we need to get much more aggressive in using this tool. The corrupt, the ineffective, and the failures need to be removed and replaced with people who will do a good job.

Joe Biden is breaking his oath of office by not protecting the border. It's an abject failure to protect America and its citizens, and it's just one thing that should cost him his job. Those who won't serve justice impartially in the DOJ and FBI, crooked federal judges, and impotent politicians need to face the consequences of their poor job performance and corruption and be removed from office. If you sleep with a Chinese spy, as Eric Swalwell did—and then lie about it—you should lose your job.[156] This man served on the House Intelligence Committee, holding our nation's secrets!

Yet, some fellow Republicans have told me to my face that they don't "believe" in impeachment, even though it's very much a part of the Constitution! To me, it's shocking that these people circle the wagons to protect their own, no matter how they've failed the American people. It leaves me feeling alone in Washington. But when I leave DC, I feel the swell of support for holding these failures accountable for their actions.

Competition drives excellence. It's at the heart of a free-market economy and capitalism. So, why are our politicians and other civil servants protected from the consequences of their actions? If we want real progress in our country, we need to begin at the top and clean house—which means holding Joe Biden accountable and impeaching this man for his crimes against his country. That begins with the voters, and to ensure that each and every vote counts, we must enact election reforms to secure the integrity of our elections. Let's look at that in the next chapter.

15

Lawfare

DURING THE 2022 MIDTERM ELECTIONS, some were expecting a "red wave"—an overwhelming turnout of Republican voters who would usher the GOP into House and Senate majorities. However, a few were preaching caution, warned not to get complacent and instead, treat it like a desperation moment.

There was no red wave, and Republicans barely took a slim majority in the House. And while this is enough for my fellow representatives and me to get control of important committees, it will take more than that to ensure justice is done in America.

Darren Beattie correctly anticipated that because of ongoing election law problems in key states—namely, they didn't stop absentee ballots or fix issues with the machines—and redistricting issues, Republicans would fail to see mass gains. This was despite widespread public sentiment against an ever-more radical Left and dissatisfaction with the Biden administration from failures like Afghanistan, record inflation, and an economy sliding into recession. Unaddressed, the underlying problems aren't going away, and they will continue to keep Republicans from experiencing a red wave that can demonstrate how tired the public is of the extremists in the Democrat party.

At the heart of the problem, poor election laws in certain states (Colorado, Arizona, Wisconsin, Pennsylvania, and Michigan, to name a few), create loopholes that leave these states ripe for fraud. This is made worse by the recent Supreme Court decision on redistricting, which will make some districts overwhelmingly Black and thus likely to go Democrat (even though they only want to use African Americans for their vote instead of actually helping them). These ongoing issues will have repercussions in future elections, and I don't think it's overstating to say that the country's future hangs in the balance.

I travel a lot and take the temperature of the country, but gauging elections is more than this. If the sentiment against the radical Left were all it took, we would've had our red wave; as it is, the issues are bigger than the attitudes of the American people. We also face significant questions about whether Republicans *can* even get the votes necessary to retake the Presidency and the Senate while holding onto the House.

The people want solutions to issues that affect them daily, and they want the party that has the best answers to those problems. Yet, how can the GOP get the chance to deliver those answers when issues like election fraud are stacked against us, and we're ridiculed for bringing up the obvious problems?

Election Reform

One of the biggest problems facing our country is election fraud, and to me, absentee ballots are the worst offenders. While the Left and their mouthpieces in the media have made every effort to mock and discredit anyone who questions election integrity, the fact is that Joe Biden won Georgia by fewer than twelve thousand votes.[157] Those who bothered to try were able to verify that voter fraud did, in fact, occur, but the consensus (at least among the legacy media) was that it wasn't "enough" to change the results. Yet, the fact remains that dead people such as Deborah Jean Christiansen, James Blalock, and Linda Kesler of Nicholson—the last two having died many years ago—still voted in Georgia.[158]

So, how did these votes manage to make it through, and how many others did we simply not catch? The weak spot here is not the machines; it is absentee ballots. And no one can tell me differently because my ex-husband, Perry, was a victim of voter fraud.[159]

I testified under oath, "We saw a tremendous amount of voter fraud. We have investigations going on right now in Georgia. There is an investigation going on in multiple states. My husband showed up to vote, and when he went to vote, he went in person, he was told he had already voted by absentee ballot when, in fact, he had never requested an absentee ballot."[160] He wasn't alone, yet fraud deniers have owned the narrative.

The vote in 2020 was riddled with problems, many stemming from COVID. Some states, without a vote of their legislature, changed their election laws because of the pandemic. Since most of these changes occurred without an official vote, these changes may be unconstitutional. Secretary of State Brad Raffensperger defied our state election laws and allowed for mass absentee ballots in Georgia. He mailed every single registered voter in the state of Georgia a form so that they could request an absentee ballot. And then, if they asked for one, they could vote by mailing in their absentee ballot for the primary, runoff, and general elections of 2020.

Only my ex-husband Perry didn't request an absentee ballot. When he showed up for early in-person voting, he was told he *could not vote* because *he already had*. Except, he hadn't!

"I'm sorry, Mr. Greene," they told him, "you've already voted by absentee ballot."

He told them, "No, I haven't. I never even requested an absentee ballot. I'm voting in person."

"We have it right here on the Secretary of State website," they told him. They turned the computer around so he could see the screen.

"Well, that's wrong," he explained. "I have not requested and never have requested an absentee ballot." He argued with them over it and was adamant that it was a mistake.

"You can go over to that line," they told him, "and sign an affidavit that you will surrender your absentee ballot, and then you can vote in person."

Over in the other line—there was a *line!*—people had the same story as Perry. He was mad and knew exactly what was going on: election fraud. Standing there with other people with similar experiences, Perry knew someone was cheating the system with these absentee ballots. He had a sinking feeling as he realized how bad this was.

No one in line he talked to had asked for an absentee ballot either. It wasn't just Perry; this was a whole group of people.

Perry signed his affidavit and wrote that he had never asked for or filled out an absentee ballot. Yet, he couldn't "surrender" the absentee ballot because he never received it. Fortunately, he was able to vote in person, but I can imagine how many other people may not have stayed around to wait in the other line.

When I told Perry's story publicly, everyone accused me of lying. The legacy media attacked me, calling me a conspiracy theorist. Even the Floyd County Elections Board said Perry was lying. Yet, we weren't going to take this lying down and got an attorney to make a Freedom of Information Act (FOIA) request after the election. They told us it would take a while because they were overwhelmed with finishing the election (where President Trump lost by less than twelve thousand votes).[161]

We had to wait months, but we knew what they'd find when they looked through all the forms—there was no completed absentee ballot request form with Perry's name on it. They kept the envelopes separate from the forms and could not find an envelope with Perry's name on it. Because he never requested it. They only discovered his affidavit, where he'd written at the top that he'd never requested an absentee ballot.[162]

Some questions for which I demanded answers remain a mystery because no one can explain why the Secretary of State's website listed that he had requested and turned in an absentee ballot. What happened to that ballot? Was that vote counted, and for whom was it cast? There's no way of telling because of laws protecting voters' privacy. How many other people did this affect? How did it happen in the first place? Was it human error? Was it a computer system doing something crazy?

No one can tell me that election fraud wasn't happening in the 2020 election because we experienced it *first-hand*. Thanks to the FOIA request, the Floyd County elections representatives verified our claims. We weren't lying.

Perry wasn't alone—this happened to a lot of other people. Voters from all over the state complained about this and said it happened to them, but we were the only ones I know of who made a FOIA request.

There can be no doubt or confusion in an election decided by so few votes. And while I'm vilified in the media and elsewhere as a conspiracy theorist for questioning the integrity of our elections and voting laws, I know what we experienced, and I will *not* be silenced. Our election laws must be updated to make any kind of fraud impossible.

Turnout Becomes Turnaround

I previously mentioned that one of the most powerful things Republicans can do is simply get out and vote. This is so much more important if we consider that election fraud may be taking place. How many other people had an experience like Perry's but perhaps don't know about it? If they didn't vote, they wouldn't know.

I was recently told that only 17 percent of registered voters voted in one of my counties. It's a Republican county, so it might not be a crisis, but it's an alarming number. And if it's happening in my districts, it's happening all over the country.

If a majority of registered Republicans turned out to vote, there's no way the Democrats could win. What would happen if 90 percent showed up on election day? It would be impossible for the Democrats, even if they did cheat. Yet, some of our country's most patriotic, conservative people—flag-flying, MAGA hat-wearing Americans—don't vote. They'll get on social media to complain about injustice or spar over issues, but come election day, they don't think it matters, and they stay home. What would have happened if Perry had stayed home?

This is a serious problem, and it is costing us our country! We are losing this nation because not enough conservative Christian voters are in the polls influencing the course of our nation through their votes. It blows my mind, and it's incredibly frustrating. People complain that the GOP isn't doing enough, yet many of our best people aren't registered to vote. And those who are often don't turn out.

Let me put it plainly: you don't get to complain about the direction of our country if you're not in the voting booth trying to change it. If all the patriotic, godly people in America would stand up, we could stop the insanity!

I support reforming our elections, but if Conservative voters and patriotic Americans don't turn out to vote, it won't matter. We must get people to engage and see how desperately their country needs them.

We used to think that the pendulum would always swing back and forth, left and right, between Democrats and Republicans, with the people growing tired or complacent with one side and momentum shifting to the other. But America is increasingly uniparty—the party of money and control. Democrats are doing all they can to break the pendulum because they're no longer an American political party.

The Democrats are a *communist* party.

Democrats don't play by the same rules Republicans do; in fact, they increasingly don't have to abide by *any* rules. Joe Biden and his family have gotten by with crime and corruption, yet no one holds them accountable. Hillary and her classified emails.[163] Biden administration censorship. Democrat COVID shutdowns.[164] Big-tech collusion with big government.[165] When a group has gained so much power that they control institutions like the Department of Justice, the FBI, the IRS, and others, we shouldn't be scared—we should be *terrified*.[166]

Every election should feel like a do-or-die situation for Republican candidates and voters. Am I exaggerating? I don't think so. Democrats want abortion to be codified into law,[167] and they want it available up until the day of birth! So, yes, people are getting murdered—that's life and death!

And what about the quality of life for all the children the Democrats want to disfigure? In promoting "gender-affirming care," they're cutting off breasts, mutilating genitals, and pumping under-age children full of chemicals to suppress their natural hormones, which research shows has *dire* long-term health consequences. The medications used for blocking puberty, such as gonadotropin-releasing hormone (GnRH) agonists, have many warnings; some are the same drugs developed for treating cancer and chemical castration. Warnings include the potential to cause pseudotumor cerebri, an increase in pressure inside the skull with similar symptoms of having a brain tumor![168] And they're injecting this into young children who cannot smoke or drink . . . because they think they want to be another gender today. What about tomorrow or next year? What about ten or twenty years from now, when they're living with all the health consequences of a decision they were too young to understand? Ask de-transitioners like Chloe Cole about the horrors she went through, or the suicides that happened because of the treatments and instability plaguing these poor people.[169]

And if you want to talk about potential deaths, let's talk again briefly about Ukraine, which Joe Biden and the democrats are so obsessed with, you would think they wanted to make it the fifty-first state. Biden has a deeply compromised, corrupt connection with Ukraine and Zelenksyy because of Hunter and Burisma. America has become increasingly embroiled in a war that's not our business with an unstable nuclear power, Russia. The more we support the war instead of brokering peace, the more people die—and the closer we get to a WWIII scenario. Zelenksyy is doing all he can to drag us into this war, demanding more and more weapons that are depleting our reserves and endangering our national defense.[170] I would say he's even holding President Biden hostage because of the political favors and corruption that tie them together. Lives are definitely at stake.

I'm also not exaggerating the life-or-death consequences for the hundreds of people who die daily or are reduced to basically zombies from fentanyl illegally entering our wide-open southern border. It's not hyperbole for the people who are victims of crimes committed by illegal aliens who shouldn't even be in our country. For those people, the results of our votes are incredibly important. Not only could we take steps to keep them safe, but we can also hold those accountable who are criminally endangering them with their open-border policies.

Republicans must see exactly what kind of fight this is. The stakes are higher than ever because the Democrat Party has become the party of communism. The foundation of our country is cracking as we speak, and we're on the verge of crumbling. It's just a matter of time. It *will* happen if good people continue to do nothing.

Lawfare

People ask me all the time, "What can I do?" Of course, the biggest thing is to vote—to recognize the importance of every single election. Get involved at any level you can, from the school board to your neighborhood. Bring your conservative Christian values with you, and don't be silent—speak up! Stand up for what's right.

But I'm also looking at another angle because the Democrats have had a playbook for years, and they've executed those plays while Republicans have been disorganized and stuck playing defense. It's time we analyze that playbook, learn their plans, and start beating the Democrats at their own game. We should never stoop to cheating, but there are so many things that we *can* do!

Let's call it "lawfare," because one of our best paths forward is warfare against the extremists on the Left in the courts. With a conservative Supreme Court, we've seen what can happen. We've seen significant victories in Roe v. Wade, affirmative action, and free speech. We have seen that justice can still occur in our courts, and we're seeing the lasting positive results of how many appointees President Trump made while in office.[171] While you may not be able to get a fair trial if you're a conservative in places like DC and New York, the rule of law still holds in many districts.

We need brave attorneys who will take on risks to challenge unconstitutional policies in court. We need lawyers who will change the way they look at things and push the legal limits by coming up with creative ideas to preserve law and order in our country. Democrats are perverting justice, and if we're going to stop them, we must take risks. We need the best legal minds in the country to work within the system to fix it because, right now, we have two standards of justice: one for Democrat elites and another for everyone else. In our country, if you have enough money and power, you own the system and don't have consequences, and this cannot stand. We must hold people accountable, whether rich or poor, because our country cannot endure the loss of equal justice under the law.

Our country has election laws for a reason. They're designed to preserve the integrity of the system, ensure fairness, and prevent and punish corruption. But they have flaws, and our enemies are smart and savvy. They've been working the system to their advantage for many years.

It's time to take it back. It's time for Republican voters to stand up and be counted, to push back against the extremes of the Democrat party that are poisoning our country. We've been silent too long, playing nice while the Left goes for blood. They have worked the system against us, and even the justice that has defined our country for many years is in jeopardy. I urge you to go out and vote—make your values known. Don't let them lull you with apathy or convince you it doesn't matter or that the pendulum will swing on its own. We can take nothing for granted, and the course of our country is in our hands.

So, what will *you* do with it?

16

What Is the GOP Doing?

Everywhere I go, whether it's back home or on the road, people ask me, "Why isn't anything happening?" They want to know why the Democrats are getting by with so much and why we aren't holding them accountable. I think that's the question we're *all* asking because, for too long, the Democrat elites of this country have gotten by with whatever they want. The American people are right to demand that their leaders step up and hold everyone accountable to the same standard: the rule of law.

I answer everyone who asks me that I'm as frustrated as they are! If it were up to me, we'd be doing all kinds of things to counter the Left's America-last agenda. So, in this chapter, I have a chance to give the kind of detailed answer I'm rarely able to give when asked this question on the spot. I'd like to provide you with an inside look at how hard it is to get things done with the current thin majority and what can be done to get the kinds of representatives in government who will push wholeheartedly for the changes the American people demand.

As a business owner, I'm used to being a problem-solver. Any time my business had a problem, it was my job to find a solution, and I look at my current position the same way. It's not my job to make friends; I'm in Congress to do *work* and move forward with the will of the people of my district.

In my business, if there were an issue with a supplier, we'd look for another one who could get us what we needed so we could get the materials to our job site and get the job done to serve our customers more quickly. If we had labor problems, we'd fire underperforming subcontractors or employees so we could bring in the teams who could get the jobs done and exceed expectations. That's how it works in business—if something isn't working, you change it.

But that is *not* how things work in government. In Congress, it's extremely difficult to solve a problem. Some of this is the smart planning of our Founding Fathers, knowing that big government crushes the people. But some is the dysfunction of Washington and needs to come to light.

Building Consensus

People need to remember that House of Representatives is made up of 435 members. Imagine it as though there were 435 board members of a large company, each having an equal share or representation on the board. To pass a bill or resolution—anything—on the House floor, you must get at least 218 of the 435 people to agree.

Republicans and Democrats divide up those 435 seats, so you're not just trying to get consensus from a majority of the members; you've also got to contend with the political agendas of the two parties. As I write this, Republicans have a slim majority in the House—222 to 212 with one vacancy—but consider that if we need 218 and have even a few dissenters within the GOP, we may not get the votes required for even simple things.

You would think things like passing a farm budget would be less political and more fiscal and practical, but I've learned it's not. The game of politics infects every aspect of the process, meaning that it's not enough to have the numbers and logic about what needs to be done—say, cutting spending so we don't add to the debt. Instead, just to get something as simple as a farm bill vote, you must still account for the politics of the situation.

Americans love our farmers because we love to eat food! Our farmers grow the best food in the world, and we want them to be profitable. But even more than that, food security is national security! Whether it's corn or wheat, beef, or chicken, we want these people to succeed. So, you would think that a farm budget would be easy to pass because we wouldn't have any divide over how to make farmers successful at providing food for America (and the world). But I've learned that the Democrats bring woke identity politics into everything! They want to give special favors based on the color of the farmers' skin, their gender, and so forth. To me, we should just look at them as farmers—as Americans. None of those details change what the farmers raise and should have nothing to do with a farm bill. However, the Democrats bring these things in, and we must deal with them. It turns out we must fight on everything, even topics that should be relatively free of politics, and this gets considerably trickier when you realize that the Republican party is not always united.

I am all about the Republican base. I've met more of them than most representatives as I have traveled the country attending Trump rallies and other GOP events. I feel like I'm in tune with that base because I am one of them. I listen to their concerns, what they want for the country, and the policies they favor. Whether they're in Georgia or Oregon, Maine or California, the core Republican base is always the same. They don't change.

While the base stays the same, the representatives in more moderate districts are where we run into problems. Some may be from areas Biden won, which we might even call a D+1 district but with a Republican representative. These Republicans in Congress are often unwilling to vote for America-first or MAGA policies or take solid conservative stances on hard-hitting issues that matter the most to the GOP base. They usually won't go near controversial issues they feel may threaten their ability to get re-elected, and this is becoming a big problem with only 222 Republican members.

For instance, consider the idea of expunging President Trump's impeachments. Elise Stefanik and I have partnered together, and each of us has an expungement resolution. My resolution would expunge President Trump's first impeachment and Elise his second; these were political witch hunts the Democrats used to smear President Trump and hurt his reputation. They were also procedurally done incorrectly. The rules that young attorney Hillary Clinton helped write for the planned impeachment of President Nixon,[172] which ironically were used during President Clinton's impeachment, were not used for President Trump. Nancy Pelosi threw those rules, which were pretty good, out both times. As a matter of fact, she sent it through so fast that she did everything wrong.

Yet, Don Bacon from Nebraska has already said that he doesn't think he'd vote for expungement—it's in the past, he says.[173] "It is what it is," he said. "It happened."[174] He has no interest in correcting the record. Why undo it? Because these are outrageous wrongs! So, of the 222 Republican members of Congress, we're down to 221.

Further, Dan Newhouse and David Valadao, two of the ten Republican members of Congress who voted to impeach President Trump regarding the events of January 6, are unlikely to vote for expungement.[175] So now we're down to 219. Some other members, such as those New York Republicans who seem to balk at anything they consider risky, may also vote no. And so, very quickly, you find that even though the GOP holds a small majority, these representatives can derail what the party would like to do.

This is just one example of how incredibly frustrating it is to try to get anything done. My constituents don't understand, and I don't either. Most of these Republicans claim they won't be able to get re-elected if they vote on these contentious topics, but Elise Stefanik is also from New York, and she's not just voting for it but sponsored legislation to do it!

Perhaps ten years ago, I could see their point. But today, we face a Democrat party that has gone full-on communist, abuses its power, is corrupt, and wields the strength of the federal government, FBI, DOJ, CIA, and IRS. And they are using those forces to hurt their enemies, punish those who oppose them, and pervert our justice system to suit their whims. If there were a time when Republicans needed to stand together against the Left's tyranny, this is it!

The conservative base is ready; they see the problems and want change. Yet over and over, I and other conservatives fighting for an America-first, MAGA agenda must come home to our districts full of frustration and impotence because the rest of our party won't get things done. We have to tell our voters that we haven't been able to get a bill to the floor or vote down the Democrat's latest crazy proposal. Even though we have the majority, we have representatives who won't take a stand because they're afraid it might make them unpopular and cost them reelection.

It's not just a failure to our conference that we can't get things done; it's a failure to our country. People are beside themselves, angry that there's a criminal sitting in the White House who has no business being there or having even gotten elected in the first place. Remember, the FBI had information from that unclassified 1023 form from their top informant before the general election. Remember, Bill Barr, who was Trump's Attorney General in the Department of Justice (and a traitor), did *nothing* with it. He should have brought charges against Joe Biden based on this information alone and conducted an investigation then. We had seventeen audio recordings proving Joe and Hunter each took a *million-dollar* bribe from the Ukrainian oligarch that owns Burisma, but Barr was a coward who refused to do anything about it.

This is why the Republicans are struggling to get anything done—fear. Fear of consequences. Fear of reprisal. Fear of lost influence. It paralyzes everyone from Republican members of Congress to administrative officials to special office holders to attorney generals. These people are responsible for not doing the right thing, and their inaction costs us all.

Every Vote Matters

A lot of people don't vote. They don't think that their vote matters. "No one's ever held accountable," they say. "No one pays for their crimes. Why does any of it matter?" As they say that, they wash their hands of Republican candidates. And, you know what? I don't blame them! It's incredibly frustrating!

So, what do we do? How do we get people involved, encourage them to vote, and hold our elected officials responsible for their actions? I believe that we must rip the veil down and show the truth of what happens in government. Remember how I forced roll-call votes? This is a prime example because Congressional representatives had no accountability for how they were voting, and when I called attention to it, I forced them to be honest with the American people, who could grade them on their voting record.

I argue that we must put these hard votes to the floor, on record. After all, that's what we're there for—to vote! Every vote must be recorded, and every representative must be called to account to the American people for how they are using those votes in our government. And, if they aren't voting the way the base wants, we must elect new representatives who *will* stand up for what's right.

If representatives are afraid to vote, they don't belong in Congress. If they're too scared of a recorded vote, they're not qualified to do the job for which their districts hired them. It's pretty simple. Voting is one of our main job responsibilities.

Some Republican members in very tight districts stay focused on getting reelected, yet their unwillingness to vote for hard-hitting issues binds the hands of the whole conference. Imagine what we could do if we had 235 or 240 Republican members of Congress! Voting for expungement or anything would be easy, even with these moderates. They wouldn't matter at all, we wouldn't be begging and pleading with them, and they wouldn't be able to demand back, "Well, what are you going to do for me?" As it is, they often hold a lot of bargaining power because they can make a list of the things they want. This puts them in positions of relative strength, and we need to change that so we can have everyone in the conference pulling together.

I dream of the day we can inspire the conservatives of this country who don't vote to come out and get engaged. When they understand why things aren't getting done, I think they'll be motivated to create change. Yes, they're mad and disappointed, but we need the *voters* to hold the government accountable.

Whatever It Takes

With how vital each representative is, I think it's time for Republicans to start stealing pages from the Democrats' playbook, and one of the first is legal ballot harvesting.[176] The Democrats have been doing it for years, and where it's okay to do it, we need to send people to the voters, such as retirement homes, to help them fill out and return their absentee ballots.

In a perfect world, we'd have one-day elections, but we don't; we have weeks of elections. And that means that Republicans need to vote when they can, so we make sure we don't get tied up in another Arizona situation where a bunch of the voting machines quit working the day of the election, and thousands get turned away without voting. For years, Republicans have resisted this idea and opposed Democrats for doing it. Still, we need to get as many votes as possible by any legal means, which means taking advantage of the system until we can improve election laws.

If people are frustrated, the best way to change it is to win back the White House and expand the majority in Congress. If we put President Trump back in office, we could fix everything. Consider that the president determines who is in charge of the DOJ, the FBI, the IRS, and so much more. We could clean house and drain the swamp that frustrates so many Americans!

Do you want to stop the Left's abuse of power? Vote! Do you want to hold the Biden crime family responsible for their corruption? Vote! Do you want to stop the insanity of the Green New Deal, mutilating children, and government censorship? We must get back in control of our country! Joe Biden will not sign our bills into law, so the GOP with a slim majority in Congress isn't enough; we need to get the right people in office because the last aspects of Trump's protection for the middle class are running out.

Consider this: the Trump tax cuts expire in 2025. When they do, we will be looking at 39 percent higher tax rates. Whichever party is in the White House and holds the majority in Congress will write the tax code after these tax breaks expire. A generation of wealth is at stake, along with the middle class. More than anything, Democrats want the estate tax (or the "death tax"), which taxes money handed down that's already been taxed once.[177] They want to tax the middle class; while elites like themselves will benefit, they'll take the money from the middle class and redistribute it to the illegal immigrants.

If taxes were the only thing at stake, it would be enough to make it obvious we must regain control of the government. People don't understand how vital it is to win the 2024 elections and beyond. And to do that, we must motivate the Republican base.

Too many important policy decisions and the direction of our country are in the balance right now. From taxes to defeating the trans agenda to holding Biden and his cronies accountable and reining in spending, we must put aside our differences and disappointments to get the right people in office—people who will vote for an America-first agenda, no matter the consequences.

It's time to demand more from the Republican party because we are the ones who must put the power back in the hands of the American people.

17

Write Your Own Story

EVERY DAY, WHEN YOU GET up in the morning, you can write your own story. With each decision you make, you are taking personal responsibility for your life. It's been said that we are the sum of those decisions, but the same thing can be said of our country. If Americans wake up interested, engaged, and take personal responsibility for our country's direction, we can make a difference—not just here on our shores but for the entire world.

The opposite is true as well. If we're lazy, disinterested, and apathetic, our country is going to reflect that. If we're more concerned with what's on social media or the news than what our country needs from us, those who are engaged and have an agenda for our nation in the Democrat party will write the narrative for us.

So, what kind of story do you want to live? Do you want it to be the one dictated by Joe Biden, Nancy Pelosi, the corrupt DOJ, the trans activists, and the radical communists of the Democrat party? Because right now, they're writing the news headlines, setting the standard of justice, defining gender and sexuality—and they make it seem that if you oppose anything they stand for, *you're* the bad, intolerant one. Do you want a story of America-last policies, sending our money and jobs overseas, crippling our economy, racking up debt, and losing our standing as the world's standard and superpower?

Or do you want something better?

Our story so far has been incredibly powerful, with a nation rising on exceptional principles of God, personal responsibility, patriotism, hard work, initiative, and generosity. We helped usher in the industrial revolution, defend freedom worldwide, defeat Hitler, win the Cold War, and pioneer life-saving medical procedures. We modeled religious freedom and showed the world what a Christian nation looked like. America is the greatest country on Earth, but the wrong people have been writing our story lately.

I don't know about you, but I want to see an American story that returns to what made us great in the first place. Our country was founded on Judeo-Christian principles that guided us and defined what kind of country we were, how we interacted with each other, and what we did in the world. The Democrats have worked industriously to destroy that foundation. Still, there are strong, compassionate, hard-working, God-fearing people throughout our country who want to see us return to our roots and what makes America so special.

I want to see an America that is free again, our speech uncensored by big-brother government, giant tech and social media companies, and Left-wing activists who want to destroy the truth so they can control the narrative. I want to see us safe again, with our border secured and the flow of deadly drugs and Mexican cartels cut off. I want justice to be blind again, the same for the wealthy elite as the poor, with everyone judged equally under the law and held accountable to the same standard. I want us to return to our conservative practices financially, socially, sexually, and more.

I am calling on not just Republicans but *Christians and God-fearing people* in this country to rise up and take a stand because the Left in this country is waging war on us, specifically. It's okay to be anything else, but if you're a Christian, you're vilified and discriminated against. They are attacking our values, our rights, and our beliefs, and they are dragging our country to destruction.

I know many people who value things like mission trips, and I love that people want to go overseas and make a difference. But I implore you to make a difference right here at home! I see homeless people every day, each needing the love of God and practical, lasting help in finding more than just food and shelter but life-changing practices that will enable them to stay off the streets. I see hurting, broken people on social media lashing out because they're angry, confused, and think that Christians are the intolerant bigots that the legacy media makes us out to be. I see children with gender dysphoria who are confused about their sexuality because they've been fed constant lies on TV and online. I see lonely people who live alone walking through life depressed and unloved. There are too many to count that need us right here at home, ranging from individuals to communities to entire cities and even states. What would happen if we brought love, hard work, and values out of our homes and churches and into the world of the hurting and needy?

If every single conservative Christian did nothing more than register and go out and vote at each election, we could utterly change our nation! Democrats would have a hard time winning, even if they cheated, and we could reinstate common-sense policies that would alter the direction of our cities, states, and country. Democrats would lose control of bankrupt cities, entire states, and gradually the nation.

I believe a vast and quiet majority still lives in the middle of this country—good, solid, hard-working people who love God and their families and work every day to try to make the world a better place. I believe that if most Americans took a hard look at it, they would, as a whole, be against abortion. If they really saw what happens to these confused children who get "gender-affirming care," they would see how harmful it is. If they looked at our economy and saw the struggles of our small companies and their owners, they would see them as family members. They would put American businesses first over any country in the world.

I believe Americans are wholly good, that they don't like being under crushing debt, drugs and criminals flowing over an open border, the murder of unborn babies, or seeing kids poisoned with hormone blockers or physically mutilated before they can legally smoke or even tattoo ink on their skin.

I also believe that Americans are tired of fighting each other. Whether we're Republicans or Democrats, rich or poor, we're tired of fighting. The current system is set up to divide with identity politics, and I want us to return to "united we stand, divided we fall." That means that no matter who we are, we must no longer turn our heads and look the other way. We can't sit on the sidelines anymore, complaining but unwilling to get involved.

We can't be passive any longer because the stakes are too high.

Within our nation, a few extremists set the narrative and drive our country to perversion, bankruptcy, and destruction. Our enemies own too much of our farmland, manufacturing, and medicine. No matter how pretty our flag is or how often we sing our national anthem, we will not continue being the land of the free and the home of the brave . . . unless we *engage*.

I said this at the beginning—I never wanted to be in politics. I hate politics! Yet, I looked around and saw that few were standing up the way I felt we needed to. I saw what President Trump did and how unsupported he was, what was happening in my town with drag queen story time, and I just could not sit idly by anymore. I'm not a politician; I am a Christian, mother, and businesswoman, and I am *just like you.*

But now, we need *you* to get involved, too. Yes, get out and *vote*, but maybe there's more that you can do, too. Your area has needs, likely at every level—and needs *you*! Your party needs you, too.

The Republican party must be the one who gets our people active and leads the way into a better future—saving America. And the only way we're going to do that is to stop fighting each other, get together, define our most important issues, and come up with a plan. We cannot save America from a distance or with theory; we must get down in the trenches, fighting for what our people care about. For too long, there's been a gap between what the American people care about and what the Republican party is doing.

My biggest goal when I ran for Congress was to push for change and force the Republican Party to be the party that reflects the values of the American people and shows unwavering dedication to our country and its citizens. While there are a few loud voices for perversion and woke politics, I am convinced that most Americans want the same things—a strong America with a thriving economy, good jobs, safety, and justice. They want factories to open or stay open, making American-made products that are the best in the world. They want to end our sons and daughters dying in foreign wars, lobbyists having more influence than constituents, and they want accountability for our politicians and other officials.

I want those things, too, to save our country and get it back on track. It's my number one goal, and I will keep fighting for it because I love America and her people—every single one of them, whether they like me or not. I think the American people are good, capable of amazing things, and are worth fighting for—that *America* is worth fighting for!

Do you?

This powerful statement is widely attributed to Edmund Burke: "The only thing necessary for the triumph of evil is for good men to do nothing." Never has this been truer for America. You, dear reader, can make a difference. You don't have to run for president or Congress because there are things you can do at home in your community that no politician can do. Get involved, be active, and bring your values and convictions to every corner of this country. You bring *hope* to America with the decisions you make every day, so let's make them count!

I urge you to please get out, exercise your right to vote, and make your voice heard. No matter how much the Democrats try to silence us, they can never stop all our voices raised together. It's time to tear the duct tape off your mouth and make yourself heard because America needs you to fight for her today!

I will be right there with you, with my sleeves rolled up, working to restore our once-great nation—and helping tell the story of America First and how she became great again.

ENDNOTES

[1] https://greene.house.gov/sites/evo-subsites/greene.house.gov/files
/evo-media-document/unusually%20cruel%20an%20eyewitness
%20report%20from%20the%20dc%20jail.pdf

[2] https://www.pbs.org/newshour/nation/biden-administration
-blocked-from-working-with-social-media-firms-about-protected
-speech#:~:text=The%20lawsuit%20accused%20the%20
administration,during%20the%20COVID%2D19%20pandemic.

[3] https://www.cbsnews.com/news/republicans-hunter-biden-laptop
-former-intelligence-officials/

[4] https://www.foxnews.com/politics/squad-amendment-fails-house-to
-restore-voting-rights-to-felons-incarcerated-individuals

[5] https://www.forbes.com/sites/brucelee/2021/01/30/did-rep-marjorie
-taylor-greene-blame-a-space-laser-for-wildfires-heres-the-response/

[6] https://www.cbsnews.com/sacramento/news/jerry-brown-pge
-wildfires-charging/

[7] https://www.cnbc.com/2018/09/12/california-governor-could-sign
-bill-critics-have-dubbed-pge-bailout.html

[8] https://ballotpedia.org/Georgia%27s_14th_Congressional_District

[9] https://thehill.com/homenews/house/3654510-house-democrat
-slams-tlaib-for-antisemitic-remarks-on-israel/

[10] https://thehill.com/changing-america/respect/diversity-inclusion
/532518-house-introduces-gender-neutral-language-in-new/

[11] https://www.edweek.org/policy-politics/joe-biden-gun-free-school
-zones-champion-busing-critic-is-running-for-president/2019/04

[12] https://www.nbcnews.com/video/bloomberg-pledges-50-million-to
-combat-gun-violence-228746819746

[13] https://www.philanthropy.com/article/michael-bloomberg-and-the
-gun-violence-prevention-movement-its-complicated

[14] https://www.washingtontimes.com/news/2023/mar/20/good-guys
-guns-stop-far-more-shootings-fbi-reports/

[15] https://www.foxnews.com/us/how-prevalent-is-mental-illness-in
-mass-shootings

[16] https://www.businessinsider.com/marjorie-taylor-greene-democrat
-marcus-flowers-lost-georgia-2022-11

[17] https://www.facebook.com/FranklinGraham/posts/i-was-watching
-cbs-news-60-minutes-sunday-night-and-saw-lesley-stahls-interview
-/773204737508456/

[18] https://thehill.com/homenews/3931545-stahl-comes-under
-criticism-for-being-too-soft-with-questions-to-greene/#:~:text
=Stahl%20comes%20under%20criticism%20for%20being%20
too%20soft%20with%20questions%20to%20Greene,-by%20
Dominick%20Mastrangelo&text=CBS%27s%20"60%20Minutes"
%20correspondent%20Lesley,which%20aired%20over%20the
%20weekend.

[19] https://www.politico.com/news/2023/01/12/additional-documents
-marked-classified-found-in-bidens-wilmington-garage-00077680
#:~:text=Lawyers%20found%20the%20Obama%2DBiden,a%20
search%20completed%20Wednesday%20night.&text=Lawyers
%20for%20President%20Joe%20Biden,to%20the%20president
%20announced%20Thursday.

[20] https://www.grassley.senate.gov/news/news-releases/grassley-obtains
-and-releases-fbi-record-alleging-vp-biden-foreign-bribery-scheme

[21] https://www.politico.com/news/magazine/2022/11/15/jfk
-assassination-files-conspiracy-fbi-00066780

[22] https://denvergazette.com/news/judge-scraps-75-year-fda-timeline
-to-release-pfizer-vaccine-safety-data-giving-agency-eight/article
_f007b8b4-ad66-59b4-a270-4709bc3e4814.html#:~:text=°%20
Partly%20Cloudy-,Judge%20scraps%2075%2Dyear%20FDA%20
timeline%20to%20release%20Pfizer%20vaccine,data%2C%20
giving%20agency%20eight%20months&text=The%20Food%20and
%20Drug%20Administration,license%20its%20COVID%2D19
%20vaccine.

[23] https://www.nationalreview.com/2021/10/pennsylvanians-are-not
-amused-by-rachel-levines-latest-promotion/

[24] https://assets.ctfassets.net/qnesrjodfi80/6bQdKPLDjyo2s0I8c60gA2
/aec7a4feb53cdd469d9c59bc3dd5cc64/swain-the_inconvenient_truth
_about_the_democratic_party-transcript.pdf

[25] https://www.senate.gov/about/origins-foundations/senate-and
-constitution/senate-passes-the-thirteenth-amendment.htm#:~:text
=On%20April%208%2C%201864%2C%20the,the%20amendment
%2038%20to%206.

[26] https://calendar.eji.org/racial-injustice/mar/06#:~:text=On %20March%206%2C%201857%2C%20in,to%20sue%20for %20his%20freedom.

[27] https://www.scotusblog.com/2023/06/supreme-court-strikes-down -affirmative-action-programs-in-college-admissions/

[28] https://abcnews.go.com/Politics/americans-approve-supreme-court -decision-restricting-race-college/story?id=100580375

[29] https://www.youtube.com/watch?v=o9e9uV8CCek

[30] https://www.ilo.org/global/about-the-ilo/newsroom/news/WCMS_855 019/lang--en/index.htm#:~:text=GENEVA%20(ILO%20News)%20 –%20Fifty,Global%20Estimates%20of%20Modern%20Slavery%20.

[31] https://nypost.com/2021/11/29/lebron-james-is-the-king-of -hypocrisy-when-it-comes-to-china/

[32] https://www.foxnews.com/media/liberals-cori-bush-ben-jerrys -attack-us-july-4th-stolen-land-gleeful-white-supremacists

[33] https://bush.house.gov/media/press-releases/bush-statement-on -ukraine-supplemental-funding-vote#:~:text="This%20evening %2C%20I%20voted%20in,of%20resolve%20and%20unrelenting %20resilience.

[34] https://www.nbcnews.com/think/opinion/ukraine-has-nazi-problem -vladimir-putin-s-denazification-claim-war-ncna1290946

[35] https://thehill.com/homenews/campaign/499128-biden-tells -charlamagne-tha-god-if-you-dont-support-me-then-you-aint-black/

[36] https://www.businessinsider.com/biden-said-desegregation-would -create-a-racial-jungle-2019-7

[37] https://www.cnbc.com/2019/06/27/harris-attacks-bidens-record-on -busing-and-working-with-segregationists.html

[38] https://www.cnn.com/2007/POLITICS/01/31/biden.obama/

[39] https://www.heritage.org/gender/commentary/how-pelosis-equality-act-would-ruin-womens-sports

[40] https://www.usccb.org/committees/religious-liberty/stopping-equality-act-key-points-and-steps

[41] https://time.com/5943613/equality-act-family/

[42] https://time.com/5943613/equality-act-family/

[43] https://www.law.cornell.edu/wex/indecent_exposure

[44] https://www.oklahoma-criminal-defense.com/crimes/indecent-exposute#:~:text=The%20penalties%20for%20indecent%20exposure,ranging%20from%20%24500%20to%20%2420%2C000.

[45] https://www.heritage.org/gender/commentary/how-pelosis-equality-act-would-ruin-womens-sports

[46] https://www.wpri.com/news/politics/auchincloss-staff-embroiled-in-disputes-involving-colbert-taylor-greene/

[47] https://www.congress.gov/bill/117th-congress/house-bill/8731/cosponsors

[48] https://nypost.com/2022/08/24/boston-childrens-hospitals-transgender-insanity-elites-profit-from-kids/

[49] https://www.markey.senate.gov/news/press-releases/sen-markey-and-rep-jayapal-introduce-the-trans-bill-of-rights-ahead-of-international-transgender-day-of-visibility

[50] https://www.snopes.com/articles/464807/minor-attracted-persons-flag/

[51] https://www.standingforfreedom.com/2021/07/gay-mens-choir-performs-song-with-the-lyrics-were-coming-for-your-children/

[52] https://nypost.com/2023/06/09/audrey-hales-parents-transfer-manifesto-to-school/, https://nypost.com/2023/03/27/nashville-cops-find-more-writings-inside-audrey-hales-car/

[53] https://www.ny1.com/nyc/all-boroughs/news/2022/06/10/study-estimates-transgender-youth-population-has-doubled-in-5-years

[54] https://www.newsweek.com/fauci-said-masks-not-really-effective-keeping-out-virus-email-reveals-1596703

[55] https://www.newsweek.com/fauci-said-masks-not-really-effective-keeping-out-virus-email-reveals-1596703

[56] https://www.thehealthyamerican.org/masks-dont-work

[57] https://www.nationalguard.mil/News/Article/2466077/dod-details-national-guard-response-to-capitol-attack/

[58] https://www.nytimes.com/2022/01/02/technology/marjorie-taylor-greene-twitter.html

[59] Marjorie Taylor Greene, @mtgreene, Twitter, 19 July 2021

[60] Marjorie Taylor Green, @mtgreene, Twitter, 11 July, 2021.

[61] Marjorie Taylor Green, @mtgreene, Twitter, 18 July, 2021

[62] Marjorie Taylor Green, @mtgreene, Twitter, 9 August, 2021

[63] https://www.cnn.com/2021/07/16/politics/biden-intel-review-covid-origins/index.html

[64] https://www.nationwidechildrens.org/newsroom/news-releases/2023/02/bridge_ruch_youthsuicide_pandemic#:~:text=Data%20suggest%20depression%2C%20anxiety%20and,to%20suicide%20risk%20in%20youth.

[65] https://www.cdc.gov/coronavirus/2019-ncov/vaccines/safety/adverse
-events.html#:~:text=Synopsis%3A%20CDC%20and%20FDA
%20safety,rate%20of%2011.1%20cases%20per

[66] https://www.rpc.senate.gov/policy-papers/democrats-wasteful-covid
-spending, https://nypost.com/2022/10/07/bidens-arp-funds-went-to
-queer-cultural-center-in-san-francisco-which-had-drag-story-hour-for
-kids/,

https://www.politico.com/news/2021/07/07/states-financial-status
-pandemic-498403

[67] https://www.independent.co.uk/news/world/americas/us-politics
/marjorie-taylor-greene-fined-mask-mandate-b1917456.html

[68] https://www.dailymail.co.uk/news/article-9862091/Cori-Bush
-threatens-Mark-McCloskeys-day-come-explosive-interview-couples
-pardon.html

[69] https://www.congress.gov/bill/116th-congress/house-resolution/109
/text

[70] https://www.commonwealthfoundation.org/2017/11/02
/inconvenient-facts-debunking-climate-alarmists/

[71] https://www.Congress.gov/bill/116th-Congress/house-resolution
/109/cosponsors

[72] https://earth.org/data_visualization/a-brief-history-of-co2/

[73] https://www.epw.senate.gov/public/_cache/files/4/a/4a86454f-4287
-4d1c-ae5f-85a01b8c78b8/7E90482A76C15A7B2D2473E6EDC9
11C0.refuting-12-claims-made-by-climate-alarmists.pdf

74 https://twitter.com/AOC/status/1127604746066583552?ref_src
=twsrc%5Etfw%7Ctwcamp%5Etweetembed%7Ctwterm%5E11
27604746066583552%7Ctwgr%5Ee9fe65914c4c2401041c08
4108d0d0603c3b2891%7Ctwcon%5Es1_&ref_url=https%3A
%2F%2Fwww.foxnews.com%2Fpolitics%2Focasio-cortez-doomsday
-claim-world-end-poll-shows-67-percent-of-dems

75 https://www.foxnews.com/politics/ocasio-cortez-doomsday-claim
-world-end-poll-shows-67-percent-of-dems

76 https://nypost.com/2021/05/01/mark-zuckerberg-priscilla-chan
-pick-up-600-acres-in-hawaii/

77 https://www.latimes.com/california/story/2019-10-29/how-do
-wildfires-start

78 https://www.wweek.com/news/2023/03/15/data-shows-fires-at
-homeless-camps-remained-a-large-portion-of-portland-blazes-last-year/

79 https://www.epa.gov/climate-indicators/climate-change-indicators
-tropical-cyclone-activity

80 https://www.drroyspencer.com/2018/09/the-30-costliest-u-s
-hurricanes-have-not-increased-in-intensity-over-time/

81 https://www.c2es.org/content/international-emissions/

82 https://www.facebook.com/bjornlomborg/photos/a.221758208967
/10157523426118968/?type=3&theater

83 https://www.wweek.com/news/2023/03/15/data-shows-fires-at
-homeless-camps-remained-a-large-portion-of-portland-blazes-last-year/

84 https://www.washingtonpost.com/climate-environment/interactive
/2023/hot-cold-extreme-temperature-deaths/#

85 https://www.congress.gov/bill/116th-congress/house-resolution/109
/text

[86] https://www.congress.gov/bill/116th-congress/house-resolution/109/text

[87] https://www.congress.gov/bill/116th-congress/house-resolution/109/text

https://www.congress.gov/bill/116th-congress/house-resolution/109/text

https://www.reuters.com/markets/commodities/chinas-lithium-hub-mining-boom-comes-cost-2023-06-15/

https://earth.org/china-plastic-pollution/#:~:text=But%20China%27s%20contribution%20to%20the,important%20water%20body%20in%20China.

[88] https://www.forbes.com/sites/christopherhelman/2021/04/28/how-green-is-wind-power-really-a-new-report-tallies-up-the-carbon-cost-of-renewables/?sh=173b657173cd

[89] https://www.forbes.com/sites/christopherhelman/2021/04/28/how-green-is-wind-power-really-a-new-report-tallies-up-the-carbon-cost-of-renewables/?sh=173b657173cd

[90] https://fee.org/articles/9-crazy-examples-of-unrelated-waste-and-partisan-spending-in-biden-s-2t-infrastructure-proposal/

[91] https://heartland.org/opinion/a-simple-reason-why-net-zero-is-impossible/

[92] https://www.greenpeace.org/international/story/50689/carbon-offsets-net-zero-greenwashing-scam/

[93] https://www.npr.org/2023/03/02/1160441919/china-is-building-six-times-more-new-coal-plants-than-other-countries-report-fin

94 https://www.whitehouse.gov/briefing-room/statements-releases
/2023/04/20/fact-sheet-president-biden-to-catalyze-global-climate
-action-through-the-major-economies-forum-on-energy-and-climate
/#:~:text=President%20Biden%20has%20set%20an,by%20no%20
later%20than%202050., https://www.unpri.org/pri-blog/the-net
-zero-transition-in-china-progress-has-been-made-but-challenges
-remain/10132.article#:~:text=China%27s%20net%2Dzero%20
transition%20pathway,of%20the%20country%27s%20transition
%20pathway.

95 https://westerncaucus.house.gov/uploadedfiles/costs_of_the_green
_new_deal.pdf

96 https://www.foxbusiness.com/politics/alexandria-ocasio-cortezs
-green-new-deal-could-cost-93-trillion-group-says

97 https://www.congress.gov/bill/116th-congress/house-resolution/109
/text

98 https://constitution.congress.gov/browse/amendment-10/#:~:text
=Tenth%20Amendment%20Rights%20Reserved%20to,respectively
%2C%20or%20to%20the%20people.

99 https://www.pbs.org/wgbh/frontline/article/healthcare-women
-afghanistan-under-taliban/

https://www.bbc.co.uk/newsround/41412980#

100 https://heartland.org/opinion/a-simple-reason-why-net-zero-is
-impossible/

101 https://trumpwhitehouse.archives.gov/trump-administration
-accomplishments/

102 https://www.nbcnews.com/politics/congress/confrontational
-maxine-waters-undeterred-marjorie-taylor-greene-criticism-chauvin
-trial-n1264534

[103] https://www.cnn.com/2018/06/25/politics/maxine-waters-trump -officials/index.html

[104] https://www.foxnews.com/opinion/qanta-ahmed-ilhan-omar-is -a-disgrace-to-islam-and-doesnt-represent-my-muslim-religion

[105] https://www.arabnews.com/node/2207061

[106] https://www.facebook.com/pillarsfund/posts/activist-linda -sarsour-and-rep-ilhan-omar-pose-for-a-photo-at-cair-nationals-25t /22750673626029771/

[107] https://www.foxnews.com/video/5495726091001

[108] https://www.foxnews.com/video/6268538170001

[109] https://www.lohud.com/story/news/politics/2018/07/02/ocasio -cortez-westchester/751333002/

[110] https://www.city-sentinel.com/news/world/biden-burisma-bribery -scheme-uncovered-rep-marjorie-taylor-greene-makes-it-public-mtg -lays-it/article_65a417de-0632-11ee-bf12-d35f25f8a81b.html

[111] https://www.cfr.org/article/how-much-aid-has-us-sent-ukraine-here -are-six-charts#:~:text=Since%20the%20war%20began%2C%20the ,Economy%2C%20a%20German%20research%20institute.

[112] https://www.cnn.com/2023/07/19/politics/oversight -committee-hearing-irs-whistleblowers/index.html#:~:text=The %20whistleblowers%20also%20told%20lawmakers,to%20Hunter %20Biden%27s%20troubled%20finances.

[113] https://www.dailymail.co.uk/news/article-12224355/I-sitting -father-Hunter-Bidens-WhatsApp-Chinese-associate.html

https://nypost.com/2023/06/22/hunter-biden-used-joe-as-leverage-in -china-biz-deal-text/

[114] https://www.foxnews.com/politics/biden-repeatedly-denied
-discussing-business-deals-hunter-evidence-suggests-otherwise

https://www.foxnews.com/politics/devon-archer-confirms-joe-biden
-lied-about-knowledge-hunters-business-dealings-comer-says

[115] https://www.washingtonpost.com/technology/2022/03/30/hunter
-biden-laptop-data-examined/

https://www.cbsnews.com/news/republicans-hunter-biden-laptop
-former-intelligence-officials/

[116] https://www.foxnews.com/politics/hunter-biden-linked-account
-received-5-million-days-threatening-messages-sitting-here-father

[117] Schweizer, Peter. Profiles in Corruption (p. 55). Harper. Kindle
Edition.

[118] Schweizer, Peter. Profiles in Corruption (p. 55). Harper. Kindle
Edition.

[119] https://oversight.house.gov/release/hearing-wrap-up-irs
-whistleblowers-expose-how-bidens-were-treated-differently%EF%BF
%BC/

[120] https://www.youtube.com/watch?v=UXA--dj2-CY

[121] https://www.congress.gov/116/meeting/house/110331/documents
/HMKP-116-JU00-20191211-SD067.pdf

[122] https://www.wsj.com/video/opinion-joe-biden-forced-ukraine
-to-fire-prosecutor-for-aid-money/C1C51BB8-3988-4070-869F
-CAD3CA0E81D8.html

[123] https://www.Congress.gov/116/meeting/house/110331/documents
/HMKP-116-JU00-20191211-SD067.pdf

124 https://oversight.house.gov/release/hearing-wrap-up-irs-whistle blowers-expose-how-bidens-were-treated-differently%EF%BF%BC/

https://www.youtube.com/watch?v=UXA--dj2-CY

https://www.congress.gov/116/meeting/house/110331/documents /HMKP-116-JU00-20191211-SD067.pdf

https://www.wsj.com/video/opinion-joe-biden-forced-ukraine -to-fire-prosecutor-for-aid-money/C1C51BB8-3988-4070-869F -CAD3CA0E81D8.html

125 https://www.foxnews.com/politics/hunter-biden-linked-account -received-5-million-days-threatening-messages-sitting-here-father

126 https://nypost.com/2020/01/18/how-five-members-of-joe-bidens -family-got-rich-through-his-connections/

https://oversight.house.gov/blog/joe-biden-lied-at-least-15-times- about-his-familys-business-schemes/

127 https://nypost.com/2022/07/27/hunter-bidens-biz-partner-called -joe-biden-the-big-guy-in-panic-over-laptop/

https://oversight.house.gov/release/hearing-wrap-up-irs-whistleblowers -expose-how-bidens-were-treated-differently%EF%BF%BC/

https://www.washingtonpost.com/politics/2022/03/30/hunter-biden -china-laptop/

128 https://www.axios.com/2023/07/19/hunter-biden-joe-ziegler -whistleblower-irs-doj

https://www.foxnews.com/opinion/irs-whistleblowers-reveal-whos -blame-shocking-biden-corruption

129 https://www.foxbusiness.com/media/larry-kudlow-clear-garlands -doj-protecting-hunter-biden

[130] https://oversight.house.gov/release/hearing-wrap-up-irs
-whistleblowers-expose-how-bidens-were-treated-differently%EF%BF
%BC/

https://www.youtube.com/watch?v=UXA--dj2-CY

https://www.congress.gov/116/meeting/house/110331/documents
/HMKP-116-JU00-20191211-SD067.pdf

https://www.wsj.com/video/opinion-joe-biden-forced-ukraine
-to-fire-prosecutor-for-aid-money/C1C51BB8-3988-4070-869F
-CAD3CA0E81D8.html

[131] Schweizer, Peter. Profiles in Corruption (p. 55). Harper. Kindle
Edition.

[132] https://www.judicialwatch.org/hunter-biden-flights/

[133] https://www.wsj.com/articles/joe-bidens-second-basement
-campaign-white-house-election-2024-voting-rights-abortion
-a44b88de

[134] https://www.skynews.com.au/world-news/united-states/creepy-joe
-biden-sniffs-childrens-hair/video/e92488b99f6a87ef9e6da1f13c13
5ee2

[135] https://www.foxnews.com/politics/child-remind-biden-which
-country-last-visited-cant-remember

[136] https://www.foxnews.com/politics/biden-directed-stage-child-toys
-tots-remarks

[137] https://nypost.com/2023/04/26/biden-cheat-sheet-shows-he-had
-advance-knowledge-of-journalists-question/

[138] https://newrepublic.com/post/174292/embarrassing-jim-jordan
-fox-news-hit-hunter-biden

[139] https://www.cnn.com/2022/05/03/politics/joe-biden-abortion
-draft-opinion/index.html

[140] https://burchett.house.gov/media/press-releases/house-democrats
-block-burchett-amendment-prevent-tax-funded-transgender

[141] https://oversight.house.gov/release/icymi-former-ag-barr-refutes
-democrats-lies-that-biden-bribery-investigation-was-closed%EF%BF
%BC/

[142] https://www.grassley.senate.gov/news/news-releases/fbi-possesses
-significant-impactful-voluminous-evidence-of-potential-criminality
-in-biden-family-business-arrangements

[143] https://www.grassley.senate.gov/news/news-releases/fbi-possesses
-significant-impactful-voluminous-evidence-of-potential-criminality
-in-biden-family-business-arrangements

[144] https://www.congress.gov/bill/117th-congress/house-resolution/57
#:~:text=Specifically%2C%20the%20resolution%20sets%20forth,of
%20a%20foreign%20nation%20and

[145] https://www.grassley.senate.gov/news/news-releases/grassley-obtains
-and-releases-fbi-record-alleging-vp-biden-foreign-bribery-scheme

[146] https://www.fraserinstitute.org/article/afghanistans-rare-earth
-element-bonanza#:~:text=However%2C%20the%20resources
%20Afghanistan%27s%20land,worth%20upwards%20of%20%241
%20trillion

[147] https://www.latimes.com/world-nation/story/2022-11-17/china
-interest-afghanistan-trade-economics-stabilization

[148] https://www.nbcnews.com/politics/congress/marjorie-taylor-greene
-introduces-biden-impeachment-articles-rcna85098

[149] https://www.voanews.com/a/usa_biden-signs-executive-orders -reversing-trump-immigration-policies/6201520.html

[150] https://www.newsweek.com/under-joe-biden-undocumented -children-missing-1812728#:~:text=For%20example%2C %20in%20April%202023,missing%20under%20the%20Biden %20administration.%22

[151] https://www.city-sentinel.com/news/world/biden-burisma-bribery -scheme-uncovered-rep-marjorie-taylor-greene-makes-it-public-mtg -lays-it/article_65a417de-0632-11ee-bf12-d35f25f8a81b.html

[152] https://www.city-sentinel.com/news/world/biden-burisma-bribery -scheme-uncovered-rep-marjorie-taylor-greene-makes-it-public-mtg -lays-it/article_65a417de-0632-11ee-bf12-d35f25f8a81b.html

[153] https://thefederalist.com/2023/06/13/grassleys-17-recordings -bombshell-brings-bidens-and-burisma-back-into-the-spotlight/

[154] http://www.cnn.com/SPECIALS/multimedia/timeline/9809/starr .report/grounds/g1.htm

[155] https://constitution.congress.gov/browse/essay/artII-S4-4-7/ALDE _00000695/

[156] https://nypost.com/2023/04/19/marjorie-taylor-greene-says-eric -swalwell-slept-with-chinese-spy/

[157] https://www.npr.org/sections/live-updates-2020-election-results /2020/11/19/936647882/georgia-releases-hand-recount-results -affirming-bidens-lead

[158] https://www.foxnews.com/opinion/tucker-carlson-2020 -presidential-election-voter-fraud-dead-voters

159 https://www.valdostadailytimes.com/news/analysis-greenes
-husband-made-no-absentee-request-contradicts-records/article
_948dafc8-3500-11ed-877a-7fca217df6d4.html

160 https://www.dailycitizen.news/news/local_news/new-analysis
-indicates-rep-greenes-husband-didnt-request-2020-absentee-ballot
-contradicts-records/article_91ec342a-3559-11ed-a035-dbfec90755e5
.html

161 https://www.valdostadailytimes.com/news/analysis-greenes
-husband-made-no-absentee-request-contradicts-records/article
_948dafc8-3500-11ed-877a-7fca217df6d4.html

162 https://www.valdostadailytimes.com/news/analysis-greenes
-husband-made-no-absentee-request-contradicts-records/article
_948dafc8-3500-11ed-877a-7fca217df6d4.html

163 https://www.fbi.gov/news/press-releases/statement-by-fbi-director
-james-b-comey-on-the-investigation-of-secretary-hillary-clinton2019s
-use-of-a-personal-e-mail-system

164 https://judiciary.house.gov/media/in-the-news/weaponization
-subcommittee-backs-state-lawsuit-biden-big-tech-censorship-case-un

165 https://judiciary.house.gov/media/in-the-news/weaponization
-subcommittee-backs-state-lawsuit-biden-big-tech-censorship-case-un

166 https://www.foxbusiness.com/video/6331536503112

167 https://rollcall.com/2022/10/18/biden-says-codifying-abortion
-rights-would-be-top-priority-if-democrats-keep-congress/#:~:text
=President%20Joe%20Biden%20pledged%20Tuesday,House%20
and%20Senate%20next%20year.

[168] https://1819news.com/news/item/fda-adds-new-warning-to
-commonly-used-puberty-blockers#:~:text=The%20warning
%20informs%20users%20of,those%20of%20a%20brain%20tumor.

[169] https://nypost.com/2023/07/27/detransitioner-tells-congress-her
-childhood-was-ruined-by-gender-reassignment/

[170] https://www.cnn.com/2023/07/18/politics/ukraine-critical-ammo
-shortage-us-nato-grapple/index.html

[171] https://www.voanews.com/a/recent-us-supreme-court-rulings
-what-you-need-to-know-/7162909.html#:~:text=Conservatives%20
still%20won%2C%20a%20lot&text=Similarly%2C%20on%20
student%20loans%2C%20the,authority%20to%20police%20water
%20pollution.

[172] https://www.politico.com/magazine/story/2019/09/16/hillary
-clinton-impeachment-memo-trump-228107/#:~:text=On
%20Capitol%20Hill%2C%20Hillary%20Rodham,determine
%20whether%20to%20impeach%20Nixon.

[173] https://www.politico.com/news/2023/07/20/centrists-pan
-expunging-trumps-record-as-mccarthy-denies-any-deal-00107362

[174] https://www.foxnews.com/politics/house-republicans-divided-push
-expunge-trump-impeachment

[175] https://www.npr.org/2021/01/14/956621191/these-are-the-10
-republicans-who-voted-to-impeach-trump i

[176] https://apnews.com/article/ballot-harvesting-early-voting-election
-2024-republicans-a844f375bb86b012cfba0e67b3f77fb7

[177] https://www.thune.senate.gov/public/index.cfm/2021/8/thune
-democrats-try-to-have-it-both-ways-on-the-double-death-tax